Vice President of Education: Adam Berkin
Editorial Director: Cindy Tripp
Director, Customization and Correlations: Abigail Jungreis
Project Managers: Deborah Golumbek, Sherry Pilkerton
Executive Editor: Penny Dowdy
Editors: Ruth Estabrook, Kathryn Bresnahan
Cover Design: Matt Pollock
Cover Illustrator: O'Lamar Gibson
Book Design: Jeremy Spiegel

NOT FOR RESALE

ISBN 978-1-4957-3469-4
©2017–Curriculum Associates, LLC
North Billerica, MA 01862
No part of this book may be reproduced
by any means without written permission
from the publisher.
All Rights Reserved. Printed in USA.
15 14 13 12 11 10 9 8

Table of Contents

Standards in boldface are the focus standards that address major lesson content.

©Curriculum Associates, LLC   Copying is not permitted.

Table of Contents continued

<table>
<tr><th colspan="2">Unit 2 Number and Operations in Base Ten continued</th><th>Standards</th></tr>
</table>

Standards in boldface are the focus standards that address major lesson content.

©Curriculum Associates, LLC   Copying is not permitted.

Standards in boldface are the focus standards that address major lesson content.

©Curriculum Associates, LLC   Copying is not permitted.

We use our math thinking to figure out all kinds of problems. We can even solve hard problems from real life.

There are eight math habits that help make your math thinking grow stronger.

Keep practicing! You'll learn to think like a math pro. Then you'll be ready to take on any problem.

THE 8 MATH HABITS

1 Solve problems.
Keep looking for clues until you solve the problem.

2 Think and reason.
Make sense of the words and the numbers in a problem.

3 Show and explain.
Share your math ideas to help others understand you.

4 Use math in the real world.
Solve problems in real life.

5 Choose a tool.
Decide when to use tools like counters, a pencil, or mental math.

6 Be clear and precise.
Try to be exactly right in what you say and do.

7 Zoom in and zoom out.
Look for what's the same and what's different.

8 Use patterns.
Look for patterns in math to find shortcuts.

Read more about each math habit on the pages that follow.

©Curriculum Associates, LLC   Copying is not permitted.

MATH HABIT ①

Solve problems.

Keep looking for clues until you solve the problem.

For some math problems, you may not know where to start. You may have to try more than one way to find the answer. But the answer you get should always make sense.

To solve problems

Ask Yourself

- Can I say what the problem is asking for?
- Can I ask questions to understand it better?
- Can I try a different way if I need to?

Then, Discuss with a Partner

- I made sure I understood the problem when I …
- I know my answer makes sense because …

MATH HABIT ②

MP 2 Reason abstractly and quantitatively.

Think and reason.

Make sense of the words and the numbers in a problem.

Reasoning is thinking about how ideas go together. If you know one thing, then you know another thing. Reasoning is using math rules and common sense together.

2 3 5

To use reasoning to solve a problem

Ask Yourself
- Can I use addition to solve a subtraction problem?
- Can I write an equation to find the answer to a problem?
- Can I try out my answer to see if it makes sense in the story?

Then, Discuss with a Partner
- I turned the problem into numbers when I wrote …
- I checked my answer by …

©Curriculum Associates, LLC   Copying is not permitted.

MATH HABIT ❸

Show and explain.

Share your math ideas to help others understand you.

Explaining math ideas to others helps you understand them even better. And that helps you solve other problems later. It also helps to listen to other people. You can get new ideas too!

To help explain your ideas or listen to others

Ask Yourself

- Can I use words to show how to solve the problem?
- Can I use pictures or act out the problem with objects?
- Can I ask questions to understand another person's ideas better?

Then, Discuss with a Partner

- I drew pictures to show …
- I explained my ideas when I said …

©Curriculum Associates, LLC   Copying is not permitted.

MATH HABIT ④

Use math in the real world.

Solve problems in real life.

One of the best ways to use your math thinking is to solve real problems. Words tell the story for the problem. Math can turn the words into a model, like a picture or equation.

You can use models to solve problems about shopping, sports, or … almost anything!

To solve a real-life problem

Ask Yourself

- Can I draw a picture or write an equation to show the math?
- Can I use my math model to solve the problem?
- Can I check that my answer makes sense?

Then, Discuss with a Partner

- I used a math model when I …
- I know my answer makes sense because …

©Curriculum Associates, LLC   Copying is not permitted.

MATH HABIT ⑤

Choose a tool.

Decide when to use tools like counters, a pencil, or mental math.

There are many tools to use in math. You can use a pencil to do a lot of math. Sometimes you can use counters or base ten blocks. Often you can just do the math in your head.

To choose the best tools

Ask Yourself

- Can I do any part of the problem in my head?
- Can I write the problem on paper?
- Can I use base ten blocks?

Then, Discuss with a Partner

- The tools I chose for this problem are …
- I chose these tools because …

©Curriculum Associates, LLC   Copying is not permitted.

MATH HABIT ⑥

Be clear and precise.

Try to be exactly right in what you say and do.

Everybody likes to be right when they do math. But sometimes people make mistakes. So it's good to check your work. And it's good to say exactly what you mean when you talk about your math ideas.

To be exactly right

Ask Yourself

- Can I use words that will help everyone understand my math ideas?
- Can I find different ways to check my work when I add or subtract?

Then, Discuss with a Partner

- I was careful to use the right words when I …
- I checked my answer by …

©Curriculum Associates, LLC   Copying is not permitted.

MATH HABIT ⑦

MP 7 Look for and make use of structure.

Zoom in and zoom out.

Look for what's the same and what's different.

Math has rules. Look at these problems:

$2 + 0 = 2$

$3 + 0 = 3$

Zoom out to see what's the *same* about problems.
Any number plus 0 is that number.

Zoom in to see what's *different* about problems.
The numbers added to 0 are different.

To zoom in and zoom out

Ask Yourself

- Can I see how different numbers are made from tens and ones?
- Can I see what happens when I add numbers in any order?

Then, Discuss with a Partner

- I zoomed out and used a math rule when I …
- I zoomed in and found a difference when I looked at …

©Curriculum Associates, LLC   Copying is not permitted.

MATH HABIT ⑧

MP 8 Look for and express regularity in repeated reasoning.

Use patterns.

Look for patterns in math to find shortcuts.

It's important in math to pay close attention. You might find a pattern or see a math idea.

Think about the pattern you can see when you count by tens:

    10, 20, 30, 40, 50 …

You can use the pattern to make a good guess about what comes next.

To use patterns

Ask Yourself

- Can I find a pattern in a math problem?
- Can I use math words to describe my pattern?
- Can I figure out what is next?

Then, Discuss with a Partner

- I saw a pattern in this problem when I looked at …
- I used the pattern to make a good guess when I …

©Curriculum Associates, LLC   Copying is not permitted.

Think I can use counting on.

What is **11 − 8**?
Think of it as **8 + [?] = 11**.

✏ Circle 8 in the table. Mark each box you count to get to 11.

What number do I add to 8 to get 11?

1	2	3	4	5	6	7	8	9	10
11	12	13	14	15	16	17	18	19	20

✏ How many numbers did you count on? ___1___

✏ Now you know four facts. Write the facts.

8 + _3_ = 11   11 − 8 = _3_

_8_ + _4_ = _12_   _11_ − _4_ = _8_

▶ Reflect Work with a partner.

1 Talk About It You want to count on to find 2 + 6. What number would you start with? Why?

Write About It _____

_____

_____

Think About ▶ **Using Different Strategies to Subtract**

🔍 **Let's Explore the Idea** **Use fact families and counting on.**

2 Fill in the blanks in the equation.

12 − 8 = ☐? is the same as _____ + ☐? = _____.

3 Show how to find 12 − 8 = ☐? by counting on.

4 Explain what you did in Problem 3.

_____

_____

_____

5 Fill in the blanks in the equation.

14 − 6 = ☐? is the same as _____ + ☐? = _____.

6 Fill in the number bond to find 14 − 6.

7 Explain how picturing a number bond can help you find 14 − 6 in your head.

_____

_____

_____

©Curriculum Associates, LLC   Copying is not permitted.

Let's Talk About It
Work with a partner.

8 Katie says she would not count on 9 from 2 to find 2 + 9. Do you agree? Why or why not?

_____

_____

_____

9 How would you explain to a student who missed class what you can do to subtract in your head?

_____

_____

_____

Try It Another Way Use an open number line.

10 Dana is finding 13 − 7.
She pictures this open
number line in her head.

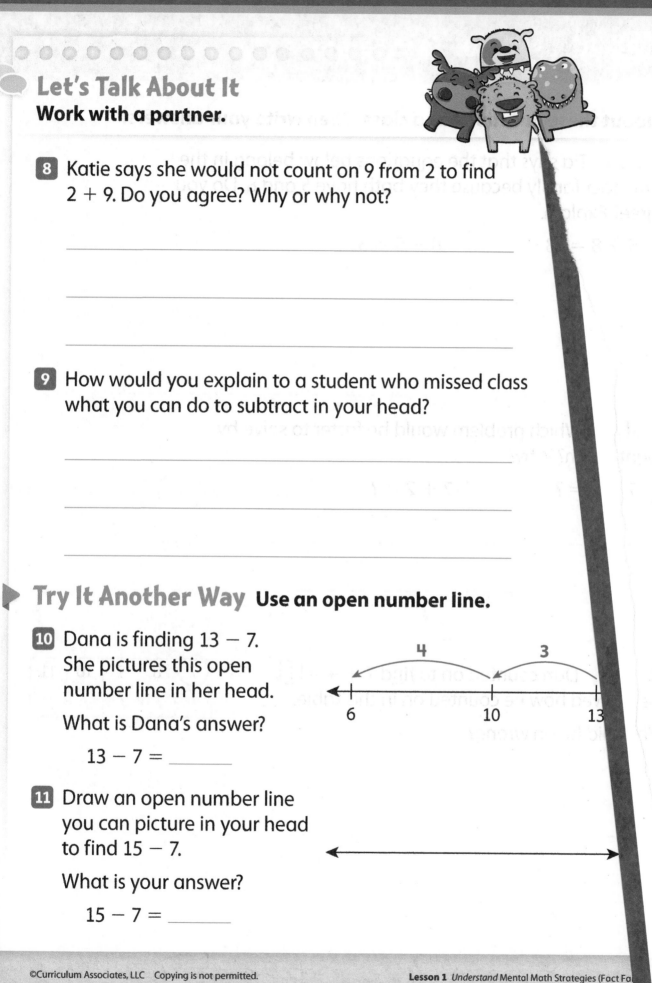

What is Dana's answer?

13 − 7 = _____

11 Draw an open number line
you can picture in your head
to find 15 − 7.

What is your answer?

15 − 7 = _____

©Curriculum Associates, LLC   Copying is not permitted.

Connect ▶ **Ideas About Fact Families**

Talk about these questions as a class. Then write your answers.

12 Explain Tia says that the equations below belong in the same fact family because they both have 5 and 8. Do you agree? Explain.

$$5 + 8 = 13 \qquad 8 - 5 = 3$$

_____

_____

_____

13 Analyze Which problem would be faster to solve by counting on? Why?

$$7 + 8 = ? \qquad 7 + 2 = ?$$

_____

_____

_____

14 Identify Dan counted on to find $7 + 4 = \boxed{?}$. He showed how he counted on in this table.

What did he do wrong?

7	8	9	10	11
/	/	/	/	

_____

_____

_____

©Curriculum Associates, LLC   Copying is not permitted.

Apply ▶ **Ideas About Fact Families**

Put It Together **Use what you have learned to complete this task.**

15 Look at these equations.

$$11 - 6 = ? \qquad\qquad 9 + 4 = ?$$

Part A Show one way you could solve $11 - 6 = \boxed{?}$.

$$11 - 6 = \underline{\qquad}$$

Part B Why did you solve the problem this way?

_____

_____

Part C Show a way you could solve $9 + 4 = \boxed{?}$ that is different from what you did in Part A.

$$9 + 4 = \underline{\qquad}$$

Part D Which way do you think you will use most often to add numbers in your head? Why?

_____

_____

_____

Solve One-Step Word Problems

🔍 Use What You Know

Solve a one-step word problem.

Seth ate 9 grapes. Then his dad gave him more grapes, and he ate them. Seth ate 15 grapes in all. How many grapes did Seth's dad give him?

a. What is the total number of grapes Seth ate? Write this number in the top box.

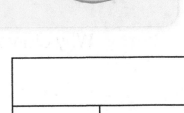

b. How many grapes did Seth eat first? Write this number in the bottom left box.

c. What does the ? stand for?

_____

_____

d. Write an equation using the numbers in the model.

_____ + ? = _____

e. How many grapes did Seth's dad give him?

_____

©Curriculum Associates, LLC   Copying is not permitted.

Connect It Use a model and equation to solve the problem.

2 What number is the total? What part do you know? Complete the model at the right.

3 Write two equations for the model.

      _____ + ? = 15   15 − _____ = ?

4 Explain what the equations show.

_____

_____

5 How many boys are on the team? Tell how you know.

_____

_____

6 **Talk About It** Why can you add or subtract to solve the problem on the previous page?

Write About It _____

_____

_____

Try It Try another problem.

7 Jen has 12 pencils. 7 are blue and the rest are white. How many white pencils does she have? Write an equation to solve.

_____

Learn About ▶ Solving Comparison Word Problems

Read the problem. Then you will explore different ways to solve word problems.

A small bag holds 3 fewer soccer balls than a big bag. The small bag holds 9 soccer balls. How many soccer balls does the big bag hold?

▶ **Understand It** You can write what you know and don't know.

Know: small bag = **9** balls

Know: small bag + **3** = big bag

Find: How many balls in the big bag?

▶ **Picture It** You can draw a picture.

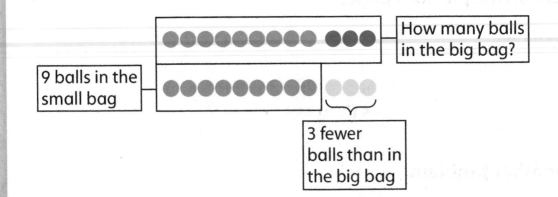

9 balls in the small bag

How many balls in the big bag?

3 fewer balls than in the big bag

©Curriculum Associates, LLC   Copying is not permitted.

▶ Connect It Write an equation to solve the problem.

8 The small bag holds _____ fewer balls than the big bag. So, the big bag holds _____ more balls than the small bag.

9 How many balls does the small bag hold? _____

10 Write an addition equation to solve the problem. What does the equation show?

_____

_____

_____

11 **Talk About It** Can you write a subtraction equation to find the answer to this problem? Explain.

Write About It _____

_____

▶ Try It Try another problem.

12 Ted has 8 white balloons and some red balloons. There are 2 fewer white balloons than red balloons. How many red balloons does Ted have?

_____

_____

Practice ▶ **Solving Different Kinds of Word Problems**

Study the model below. Then solve Problems 13–15.

Example

Jen scored 6 more points than Sue. Jen scored 13 points.
How many points did Sue score?

You can draw a picture.

Jen's points: • • • • • • • • • • • • •

Sue's points: • • • • • • • ⫽⫽⫽⫽⫽⫽

Jen's points − 6 = Sue's points.

$$13 - 6 = 7$$

Answer ___Sue scored 7 points.___

---

13 There are 14 dogs at the dog park.
There are 6 black dogs. The rest are brown.
How many brown dogs are at the dog park?

Show your work.

$$14 - 6 = 8$$

What do you know?
What are you trying
to find out?

Answer ___There are___

©Curriculum Associates, LLC Copying is not permitted.

14 Kim had 12 stickers. She gave some to her sister. Now Kim has 6 stickers left. How many stickers did Kim give her sister?

Show your work.

You can add or subtract to find the answer.

Answer _____

15 Kyle has 7 fish. He has 4 fewer fish than Ana. How many fish does Ana have?

A 3

B 4

C 11

D 12

Who has more fish?

Deb chose **A** as the answer. This answer is wrong. How did Deb get her answer?

_____

_____

_____

Practice ▸ **Solving Different Kinds of Word Problems**

Solve the problems.

1 Rick has 13 marbles. 4 marbles are blue. The rest are white. How many white marbles are there?

Fill in the blanks. Then circle the letter for all the equations that can be used to solve the problem.

A $13 - 4 = $ _____

C $13 + 4 = $ _____

B $13 - $ _____ $= 4$

D $4 + $ _____ $= 13$

2 There are 5 cows in the barn. There are 8 fewer cows in the barn than in the field. How many cows are in the field? Circle the correct answer.

A 3

C 12

B 8

D 13

3 Jin has 9 markers. He has 5 more markers than pencils. How many pencils does Jin have?

Circle *Yes* or *No* to tell if each equation can be used to solve the problem.

a. $9 - 5 = 4$ Yes   No

b. $9 + 5 = 14$ Yes   No

c. $14 - 5 = 9$ Yes   No

d. $5 + 4 = 9$ Yes   No

©Curriculum Associates, LLC   Copying is not permitted.

4 There were 4 children on a rug. More children joined them. Now there are 10 children on the rug. How many children joined the first 4 children? Circle the correct answer.

A 4

C 6

B 5

D 14

5 Write a problem that can be solved using the tape diagram at the right.

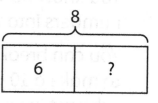

_____

_____

_____

_____

6 Show how to solve the problem you wrote in Problem 5. Then ask a partner to solve the problem a different way. Show how your partner solved it.

_____

_____

_____

_____

✓ **Self Check** **Now you can solve one-step problems. Fill this in on the progress chart on page 1.**

Lesson 3 👥 Introduction

Understand Mental Math Strategies (Make a Ten)

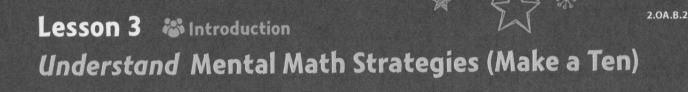

💭 Think It Through

How can you make a 10 to add and subtract in your head?

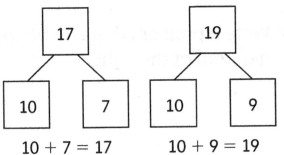

You know how to break apart numbers into tens and ones.

You can break apart numbers to make a 10 when you add or subtract in your head.

$10 + 7 = 17$ $10 + 9 = 19$

Think **You can make a 10 to add.**

Add **9 + 7**.

Think of 9 red counters and 7 blue counters on two 10-frames.

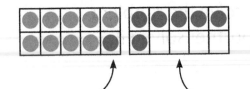

The first blue counter makes a full 10.

There are 6 more blue counters in the second 10-frame.

Add **9 + 7**.
Think of **7** as **1 + 6**.
Add **9** and **1** to make **10**.

$9 + 7$
$9 + 1 + 6$
$10 + 6$

✏️ Write the sums.

$10 + 6 =$ _____ $9 + 7 =$ _____

        ©Curriculum Associates, LLC   Copying is not permitted.

Think You can make a 10 to subtract.

Subtract 14 − 6.

Start with 14 counters.

When I have 14, I have 10 and 4 more.

Put an X over the counters in the second 10-frame. How many counters do you subtract to get to 10? _____

How many more counters need an X to subtract a total of 6? _____ Put an X over this number of counters in the first 10-frame.

Use the 10-frames to complete each equation.

14 − _____ = 10

10 − _____ = 8

Subtracting 6 is the same as subtracting 4 and then subtracting 2 more. So, 14 − 6 = 8.

▶ Reflect Work with a partner.

1 **Talk About It** How can you make a 10 to help you add 8 + 7?

Write About It _____

_____

_____

Think About ▶ **The Strategy of Making a Ten**

🔍 **Let's Explore the Idea** Use open number lines to add and subtract.

Answer Problems 2 through 4 to help you think about 8 + 8 = 16.

2 Complete the equations.

$$8 + \_\_\_\_\_ = 10 \qquad 10 + \_\_\_\_\_ = 16$$

3 Use your answers from Problem 2 to fill in the boxes on the open number line.

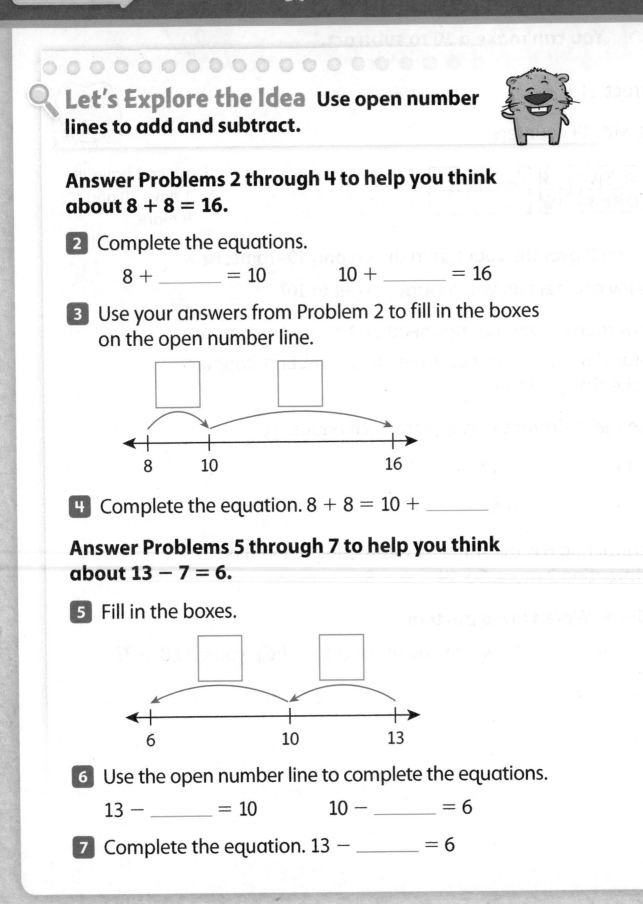

4 Complete the equation. $8 + 8 = 10 + \_\_\_\_\_$

Answer Problems 5 through 7 to help you think about 13 − 7 = 6.

5 Fill in the boxes.

6 Use the open number line to complete the equations.

$$13 - \_\_\_\_\_ = 10 \qquad 10 - \_\_\_\_\_ = 6$$

7 Complete the equation. $13 - \_\_\_\_\_ = 6$

©Curriculum Associates, LLC   Copying is not permitted.

Let's Talk About It
Work with a partner.

8 Look at the open number line in Problem 3.
Why do you add 2 to 8?

_____

Why do you add 6 next?

_____

9 Look at the open number line in Problem 5.
Why do you first subtract 3 from 13?

_____

Why do you subtract 4 next?

_____

_____

▶ Try It Another Way Use a ladder model.

Fill in the blanks to add or subtract.

10 Find 8 + 6 by adding up.

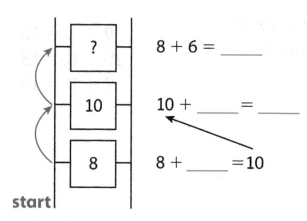

8 + 6 = _____

10 + _____ = _____

8 + _____ = 10

11 Find 14 − 6 by subtracting down.

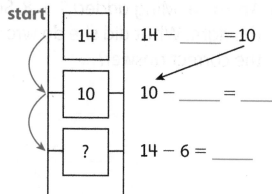

14 − _____ = 10

10 − _____ = _____

14 − 6 = _____

Talk about these questions as a class. Then write your answers.

12 Demonstrate Show how to make a 10 to find $6 + 9$. Explain your thinking.

_____

_____

_____

13 Compare Greta and Chuck each added $5 + 7$ by making a 10.

Greta $5 + 7$	Chuck $5 + 7$
Break apart 5. $2 + 3$	Break apart 7. $5 + 2$
$7 + 3 = 10$	$5 + 5 = 10$
Add 2 more. $10 + 2 = 12$	Add 2 more. $10 + 2 = 12$
$7 + 5 = 12$	$7 + 5 = 12$

Did they both make a 10 correctly? Explain.

_____

_____

_____

14 Analyze Ming added $9 + 8$. See her work at the right. What did she do wrong? What is the correct answer?

$$9 + 1 = 10$$
$$10 + 8 = 18$$
$$9 + 8 = 18$$

_____

_____

_____

Apply ▶ Ideas About Making a Ten   23

Put It Together Use what you have learned to complete this task.

15 Think about making a 10 to add or subtract.

Part A Choose two numbers you can add by making a 10. Write an addition equation using your numbers.

_____ + _____ = ?

Draw a model to show how to answer your addition problem by making a 10.
Then solve your addition problem.

_____ + _____ = _____

Part B Choose two numbers you can subtract by making a 10. Write a subtraction equation using your numbers.

_____ − _____ = ?

Draw a model you could use to solve your subtraction equation by making a 10. Then solve your subtraction problem.

_____ − _____ = _____

Part C How can making a 10 help you add or subtract in your head?

_____

_____

_____

Understand Even and Odd Numbers

2.OA.C.3

💭 Think It Through

What are even and odd numbers?

You can break apart some numbers into groups of 2. Look at these 8 socks.

Think **Sometimes when you make groups of 2, there is a leftover.**

Look at these 7 shoes.

🖊 Circle groups of 2.

🖊 How many shoes are NOT in a group of 2? _____

©Curriculum Associates, LLC   Copying is not permitted.

Think Make groups of 2 to tell if a number is even or odd.

A number is **even** if you make groups of 2 and have no leftovers.

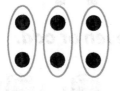

There are no leftovers, so 6 is even.

A number is **odd** if you make groups of 2 and have 1 leftover.

There is 1 leftover, so 5 is odd.

Think Try making 2 equal groups to tell if a number is even or odd.

A number is **even** if you can make 2 equal groups.

Each group has the same number, so 6 is even.

A number is **odd** if you cannot make 2 equal groups.

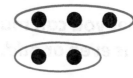

Each group has a different number, so 5 is odd.

▶ **Reflect** Work with a partner.

1 Is 9 an even or odd number? Why?

9 is odd because there is 5 +4

and

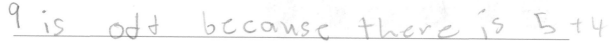

Think About ▶ **Identifying Even and Odd Numbers**

🔍 **Let's Explore the Idea** **Tell if a number is *even* or *odd*.**

Circle groups of 2. Then tell if the number is *even* or *odd*.

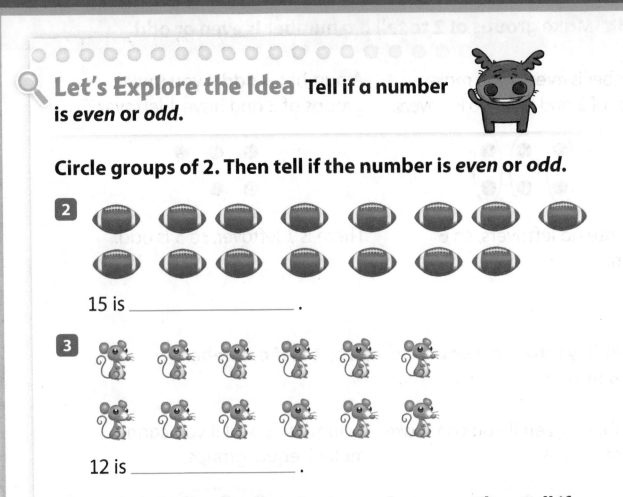

2

15 is _____ .

3

12 is _____ .

Show whether you can make 2 equal groups. Then tell if the number is *even* or *odd*.

4

14 is _____ .

5

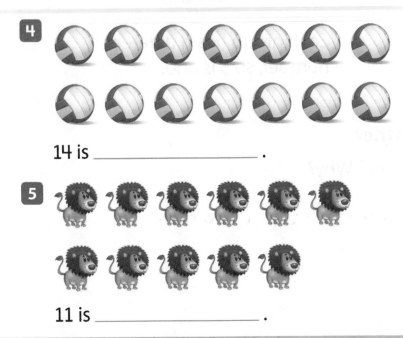

11 is _____ .

©Curriculum Associates, LLC   Copying is not permitted.

Let's Talk About It
Work with a partner.

6 Write a doubles fact for 8.

_____ + _____ = 8

7 Write a doubles + 1 fact for 9.

_____ + _____ + 1 = 9

8 Write these doubles or doubles + 1 facts.

_____ + _____ = 10   _____ + _____ + 1 = 7

_____ + _____ = 12   _____ + _____ + 1 = 15

9 Are sums of doubles odd or even numbers? Are sums of doubles + 1 odd or even numbers? Explain.

_____

_____

_____

▶ **Try It Another Way** **Skip count by 2s to find even numbers.**

You can skip count by 2s to find even numbers.

10 Skip count by 2s to finish this list. Stop at 20.

2, 4, 6, _____

11 Numbers on your list in Problem 10 are even. Numbers less than 20 that are not on your list are odd.

Circle the even numbers. Underline the odd numbers.

11   14   16   17

Connect ▶ Ideas About Even and Odd Numbers

Talk about these questions as a class. Then write your answers.

12 Evaluate Pat looks at this picture of 14 apples. He says that 14 is an odd number. Do you agree? Explain.

_____

_____

_____

13 Analyze Ms. Lane's class is in pairs. There are 9 pairs of students. There is also 1 student paired with Ms. Lane. How many students are in the class? Is the number even or odd? Explain.

_____

_____

_____

14 Explain Mimi says that when she adds doubles, the sum is always even. It doesn't matter if the doubles are odd or even numbers. Do you agree? Explain.

_____

_____

_____

©Curriculum Associates, LLC   Copying is not permitted.

Apply ▶ **Ideas About Even and Odd Numbers** 29

Put It Together **Use what you have learned to complete this task.**

15 Use this table to answer the questions.

1	2	3	4	5	6	7	8	9	10
11	12	13	14	15	16	17	18	19	20

Part A Color squares with odd numbers red. Color squares with even numbers blue. What patterns do you see in the numbers?

_____

_____

Part B Look at 15. Is the ones digit odd or even? Is 15 odd or even?

_____

Part C Look at 16. Is the ones digit odd or even? Is 16 odd or even?

_____

Part D Amy says that if a two-digit number has an even number in the ones place, the number is also even. Is she correct? Why or why not?

_____

_____

Use What You Know

Review adding 3 one-digit numbers.

Rob's team has shelves for their hats. How many hats are there in all?

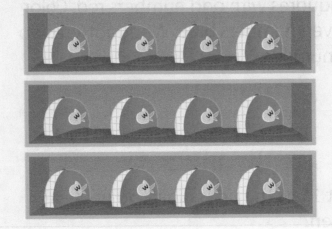

a. Does each shelf have the same number of hats? _____

b. How many hats are on each shelf? _____

c. How many shelves are there? _____

d. Look at the lines at the right. Each line shows one shelf. Use numbers to write how many hats are on each shelf.

_____

_____

_____

e. Use your answer to Problem d. Write an equation to show the total number of hats.

_____

©Curriculum Associates, LLC   Copying is not permitted.

The hats on shelves on the previous page show an **array**.
An array has **rows** and **columns**. Here is the same
array made out of dots instead of hats.

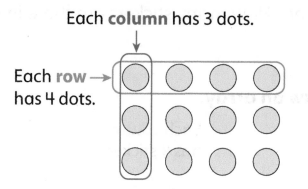

Each **column** has 3 dots.

Each **row** → has 4 dots.

In an array,

• every row has the same number of objects.

• every column has the same number of objects.

▶ **Reflect** **Work with a partner.**

1 **Talk About It** Kimi makes an array using 10 stamps.
Her array has 2 rows. How many stamps are in each column?
Explain how you know.

Write About It _____

_____

_____

Learn About ▸ **Adding Using Arrays**

Read the problem. Then you will look at ways to use an array.

> Mike puts some stickers into an array. Each row has 5 stickers.
> Each column has 4 stickers. How many stickers are there in all?

▸ **Picture It** **You can draw an array.**

Each **column**
has 4 stickers.

Each **row** has
5 stickers.

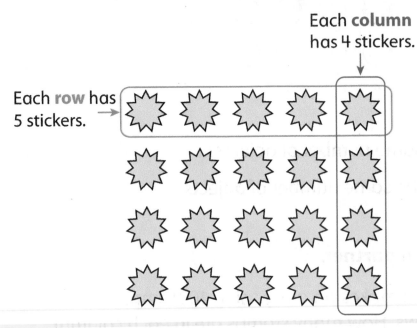

▸ **Model It** **You can use the rows in the array to write an equation.**

Add the number of stickers in each row.
Each row has 5 stickers ⟶ $5 + 5 + 5 + 5 = ?$

▸ **Model It** **You can use the rows in the array to skip count.**

There are 5 stickers in each row. Skip count by 5s ⟶ 5, 10, 15, 20.

Connect It Use the array and models to solve the problem.

2 Look at the first *Model It* on the previous page. Why is 5 written four times in the equation?

_____

3 Write an equation you could use to find the total number of stickers using the columns.

_____

4 Look at the second *Model It* on the previous page. Why do you skip count by 5s?

_____

5 **Talk About It** **Work with a partner.**

Do you need to see the array from *Picture It* to solve the problem on the previous page?

Write About It _____

_____

_____

Try It Try another problem.

6 Write two equations you could use to find the total number of shapes in this array.

_____

_____

©Curriculum Associates, LLC   Copying is not permitted.

Practice ▶ **Adding Using Arrays**

Study the model below. Then solve Problems 7–9.

Example

There are 4 rows of crayons in a box. Each row has 4 crayons. How many crayons are in the box?

You can show your work using an array.

4 rows of 4

4 columns of 4

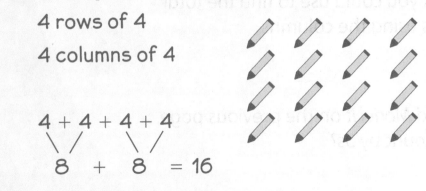

$$4 + 4 + 4 + 4$$

$$8 \ + \ 8 \ = 16$$

Answer ___16 crayons___

7 In a game, players put pieces in 3 columns. Each column holds 5 pieces. How many pieces fill all 3 columns? Draw an array as part of your answer.

Show your work.

Can you skip count to find the answer?

Answer _____

©Curriculum Associates, LLC   Copying is not permitted.

8 A package has 2 rows of soup cans. Each row has 3 cans. How many cans of soup are in the package? Draw an array as part of your answer.

Show your work.

You can add the numbers in each row or the numbers in each column.

Answer _____

9 Some students line up in 2 rows to play catch. Each row has 8 students. How many students play catch?

A 8

B 10

C 16

D 18

What number can you skip count by to find the answer?

Vic chose **B** as the answer. This answer is wrong. How did Vic get his answer?

_____

_____

_____

©Curriculum Associates, LLC   Copying is not permitted.

Practice ▶ **Adding Using Arrays**

Solve the problems.

1 Which equation shows the total number
of hearts in this array?
Circle all the correct answers.

A 6 + 6 + 6 = 18

B 3 + 3 + 3 + 3 + 3 + 3 = 18

C 6 + 3 = 9

D 3 + 3 + 3 = 9

2 Which doubles fact can you use to find
the total number of shapes in this array?
Circle the correct answer.

A 5 + 2 = 7

B 5 + 5 = 10

C 2 + 2 = 4

D 10 + 10 = 20

3 Olga draws an array of dots. The array has
3 columns. The first column has 4 dots. Which
equation can you use to find the total number
of dots? Circle all the correct answers.

A 3 + 3 + 3 = ?

B 3 + 3 + 3 + 3 = ?

C 4 + 4 + 4 = ?

D 4 + 4 + 4 + 4 = ?

©Curriculum Associates, LLC   Copying is not permitted.

4 Dana makes an array using these rules.

- The number in each row is different from the number in each column.
- There is more than one row and more than one column.

Tell if each number could be the number of objects in Dana's array. Circle *Yes* or *No* for each number.

a. 6   Yes   No

b. 17   Yes   No

c. 9   Yes   No

d. 15   Yes   No

5 Draw an array with 5 rows. Put 6 objects in each row. Show how to use doubles facts to find the total number of objects.

6 Show or explain how you can use skip counting to check your answer to Problem 5.

_____

_____

✓ **Self Check**   **Now you can solve problems using an array. Fill this in on the progress chart on page 1.**

Solve Two-Step Word Problems

2.OA.A.1

Use What You Know

You know how to solve one-step word problems.

Eve had 3 striped banners and 3 dotted banners. Then she made 7 white banners. How many banners does Eve have now?

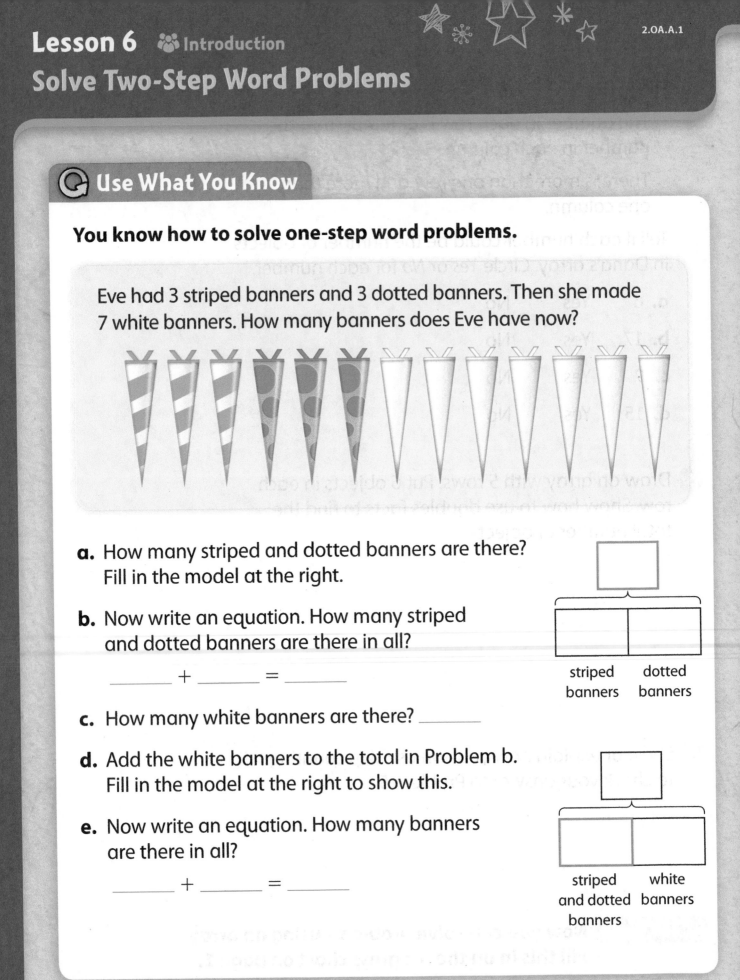

a. How many striped and dotted banners are there? Fill in the model at the right.

b. Now write an equation. How many striped and dotted banners are there in all?

_____ + _____ = _____

striped   dotted
banners   banners

c. How many white banners are there? _____

d. Add the white banners to the total in Problem b. Fill in the model at the right to show this.

e. Now write an equation. How many banners are there in all?

_____ + _____ = _____

striped   white
and dotted   banners
banners

©Curriculum Associates, LLC   Copying is not permitted.

The problem on the previous page is a two-step problem.
First, you added the striped and dotted banners.
Then you added the white banners to the sum.

Step 1: $3 + 3 = 6$ **Step 2:** $6 + 7 = 13$

Now look at this two-step problem.

Juan had 3 pink markers and 7 green markers.
He lost 2 markers. How many markers does
he have now?

Step 1: Add to find the total number of markers $3 + 7 = 10$
Juan had.

Step 2: Subtract the number of markers Juan lost $10 - 2 = 8$
to find how many he has now.

Juan has _____ markers now.

▶ Reflect Work with a partner.

1 **Talk About It** Suki had 17 grapes. She gave 8 grapes to her
sister. Then she gave 3 grapes to her friend. Would you add or
subtract to find how many grapes Suki has now?

Write About It _____

_____

_____

Learn About **Ways to Solve Two-Step Problems**

Read the problem. Then you will model a two-step problem.

Meg had 8 pears in her basket. Then she picked 6 more pears. After that, she gave away 5 pears to her friends. How many pears are in the basket now?

▶ **Picture It** **You can draw a picture.**

Step 1:   8 pears   +   6 more pears

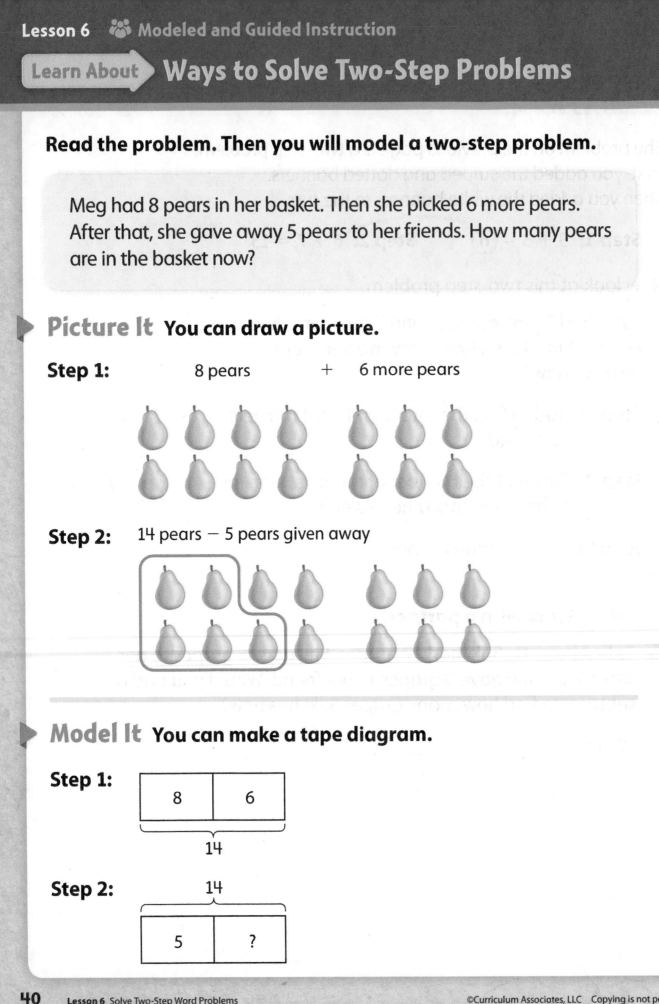

Step 2:   14 pears − 5 pears given away

▶ **Model It** **You can make a tape diagram.**

Step 1:

8	6

14

Step 2:   14

5	?

   ©Curriculum Associates, LLC   Copying is not permitted.

Connect It **Write equations.**

2 What happens in Step 1 of the problem?

_____

3 Look at *Picture It*. Write an equation for Step 1.

_____ + _____ = _____

4 What happens in Step 2 of the problem?

_____

5 Look at *Model It*. Write an equation for Step 2.

_____ − _____ = _____

6 **Talk About It** **Work with a partner.**

How is a two-step problem different from a
one-step problem?

Write About It _____

_____

_____

Try It **Try another problem.**

7 There were 12 boys in the pool. Then 3 went home.
Then 6 more boys jumped in the pool. How many boys
are in the pool now? Show your work.

_____

_____

Learn About More Ways to Solve Two-Step Problems

Read the problem. Then you will model a two-step problem.

> There were 16 quarters in a jar. Russ took 6 quarters. Then Dad added more quarters to the jar. Now there are 18 quarters in the jar. How many did Dad put in?

Picture It You can draw a picture.

Step 1: There were 16 quarters in a jar.
Russ took 6 quarters.

Step 2: Then Dad added more quarters to the jar.
Now there are 18 quarters in the jar.

Model It You can use open number lines.

Step 1: There were 16 quarters in a jar.
Russ took 6 quarters.

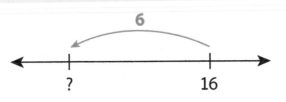

Step 2: Then Dad added more quarters to the jar.
Now there are 18 quarters in the jar.

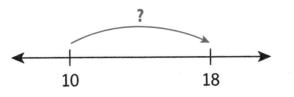

©Curriculum Associates, LLC Copying is not permitted.

> # Connect It **Understand what the models mean.**

8 What happens in Step 1 of the problem?

_____

9 Look at the number line in Step 1 of *Model It*.

Complete the equation. $16 - 6 =$ _____

10 What happens in Step 2 of the problem?

_____

11 Write an equation for Step 2.

_____ $+ ? =$ _____

12 How many quarters did Dad put in the jar? _____

13 **Talk About It** **Work with a partner.**

Explain how to solve a two-step problem.

Write About It _____

_____

_____

> # Try It **Try another problem.**

14 Gus had 7 shells. Then he found 4 more. Then some shells broke. Now Gus has 9 shells. How many shells broke? Show your work.

_____

_____

Practice ▶ **Solving Two-Step Word Problems**

Study the model below. Then solve Problems 15–17.

Example

Emma had 12 cards and Stan had 0. Stan took some of Emma's cards. Now Emma has 9 cards. How many more cards does Emma have than Stan?

Look at how you can show your work.

Emma starts with 12 cards and ends up with 9.

$12 - ? = 9$ $12 - 3 = 9$
So, Stan has 3 cards.

Emma has 9 cards. Stan has 3 cards.

$9 - 3 = ?$ $9 - 3 = 6$

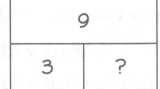

Answer _Emma has 6 more cards than Stan._

---

15 There were 6 toys in a box. Fritz took 2 toys out of the box. Then he put 8 toys into the box. How many toys are in the box now?

Show your work.

Try acting out the problem.

Answer _____

©Curriculum Associates, LLC   Copying is not permitted.

16 Rob had 16 crayons. He gave 8 crayons to Troy. Ella gave Rob some crayons. Now Rob has 17 crayons. How many crayons did Ella give to Rob?

Show your work.

How many crayons did Rob have after he gave some away? How many does he have now?

Answer _____

---

17 Bev got 6 dollars from her mom and 4 dollars from her dad. She wants to buy a game that costs 18 dollars. How many more dollars does Bev need?

A 2

B 8

C 10

D 14

How can you find how much money Bev has?

Allie chose **C** as the answer. This answer is wrong. How did Allie get her answer?

_____

_____

©Curriculum Associates, LLC   Copying is not permitted.

Practice ▷ **Solving Two-Step Word Problems**

Solve the problems.

1   Cara picked 11 big apples and 7 small apples. Dan picked 5 fewer apples than Cara. How many apples did Dan pick? Circle the correct answer.

A   18   **C**   13

B   6   **D**   2

2   There were 15 birds on a branch. Then 6 birds flew away. Then 3 birds landed on the branch. How many birds are on the branch now?

Fill in the blanks. Then circle all the answers that show a step in solving the problem.

A $15 + 6 =$ _____

B $15 - 6 =$ _____

C $9 - 3 =$ _____

D $9 + 3 =$ _____

3   Ana has 10 beads. Beth has 3 more beads than Ana. Beth has 7 small beads. The rest of her beads are big. How many big beads does Beth have? Circle the correct answer.

A   20   **C**   6

B   13   **D**   0

©Curriculum Associates, LLC   Copying is not permitted.

4 Lee had 8 square blocks and 9 triangle blocks. Jon took some of Lee's blocks. Then Lee had 10 blocks left. How many blocks did Jon take? Circle the correct answer.

A 2   **C** 17

B 7   **D** 27

5 A star card is worth 10 points. A moon card is worth 4 fewer points. How many points are a star card and moon card worth together?

Show your work.

6 Write a two-step word problem that uses addition and subtraction. Then solve the problem.

Show your work.

✓ **Self Check** **Now you can solve two-step problems. Fill this in on the progress chart on page 1.**

Use Equal Groups and Add

Study an Example Problem and Solution

Read this problem about adding to solve real-world problems. Then look at Beau's solution to the problem.

Robot Motors

Beau wants to build a shelf to store his 20 robot motors. Look at his plan.

> **Shelf Plan**
> - Use more than 1 shelf.
> - Put the same number of motors on each shelf.

How many shelves should Beau make? How many motors should he put on each shelf?

Show how Beau's solution matches the checklist.

✏️ Problem-Solving Checklist

- ☐ Tell what is known.
- ☐ Tell what the problem is asking.
- ☐ Show all your work.
- ☐ Show that the solution works.

a. **Circle** something that is known.

b. **Underline** something that you need to find.

c. **Draw a box around** what you do to solve the problem.

d. **Put a checkmark** next to the part that shows the solution works.

©Curriculum Associates, LLC Copying is not permitted.

Beau's Solution

Hi, I'm Beau. Here's how I solved the problem.

▷ **I know** I have 20 robot motors to put on more than 1 shelf. Each shelf has the same number of motors.

▷ **I need to find** how many to put on each shelf.

▷ **I can skip count** to add the same number to try to get to 20.

By 2s: 2, 4, 6, 8, 10, 12, 14, 16, 18, **20**

By 3s: 3, 6, 9, 12, 15, 18, 21, 24

By 5s: 5, 10, 15, **20**

Skip counting by 3s does not work, but 2s and 5s work.

▷ **I will try 5** motors on each shelf.

▷ **I can draw a picture** of 5 motors on 1 shelf. Then I can draw more shelves with 5 motors on each shelf.

After I drew 4 shelves I had 20 motors.

▷ **I need** 4 shelves.

▷ **Add** all the rows to check. 5 + 5 + 5 + 5 = 20.

▷ **Use 4 shelves. Put 5 motors on each shelf.**

Try ▶ **Another Approach**

There are many ways to solve problems. Think about how you might solve the Robot Motors problem in a different way.

Robot Motors

Beau wants to build a shelf to store his 20 robot motors. Look at his plan.

Shelf Plan
- Use more than 1 shelf.
- Put the same number of motors on each shelf.

How many shelves should Beau make? How many motors should he put on each shelf?

▶ **Plan It** **Answer this question to help you start thinking about a plan.**

What numbers can you use for the number of shelves? Explain how you know.

_____

_____

_____

_____

  ©Curriculum Associates, LLC   Copying is not permitted.

Solve It Find a different solution for the Robot Motors problem. Show all your work on a separate sheet of paper.

You may want to use the problem-solving tips to get started.

Problem-Solving Tips

- **Models**

Problem-Solving Checklist

Make sure that you . . .

☐ tell what you know.

☐ tell what you need to do.

☐ show all your work.

☐ show that the solution works.

- **Word Bank**

skip count	add	total
array	row	column

- **Sentence Starters**

• I can use two _____

• Each shelf holds _____ motors.

Reflect

Use Mathematical Practices Talk about this question with a partner.

• **Use a Model** What addition equations can you use to check your answer? What do they show?

Discuss ▸ **Models and Strategies**

Solve the problem on a separate sheet of paper.
There are different ways you can solve it.

Rock Collection

Beau is sorting some of the rocks in his
rock collection. He puts the rocks on the
4 trays below.

Two trays have an even number of rocks.
Two trays have an odd number of rocks.
Each tray can hold 20 or fewer rocks.

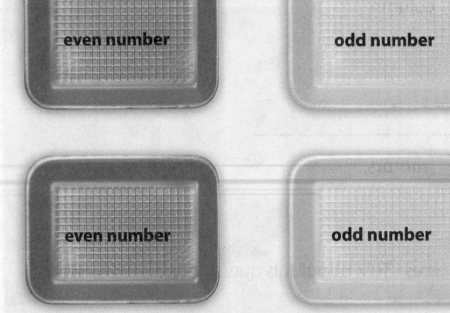

What are some ways Beau can put rocks on these
trays?

©Curriculum Associates, LLC   Copying is not permitted.

▶ Plan It and Solve It Find a solution to Beau's Rock Collection problem.

Use a separate sheet of paper.

- Write two different odd numbers and two different even numbers.
- Show how you know each number is even or odd.

You may want to use the problem-solving tips to get started.

Problem-Solving Tips

- **Questions**
  - What are the numbers I can choose from?
  - Which numbers can make equal groups?

- **Word Bank**

| odd number | equal groups | doubles |
| even number | leftover | doubles + 1 |

- **Sentence Starters**
  - I can make equal groups with _____
  - There are _____ in each group.
  - Skip count by _____

Problem-Solving Checklist

Make sure that you . . .
☐ tell what you know.
☐ tell what you need to do.
☐ show all your work.
☐ show that the solution works.

▶ Reflect

Use Mathematical Practices Talk about this question with a partner.

- **Use a Model** How can you use pictures to show that your answers make sense?

Persevere ▶ On Your Own

Solve the problem on a separate sheet of paper.

Nuts and Bolts

Beau has 18 bolts. He has 3 boxes to put them in.
He wants to put at least 3 bolts in each box.

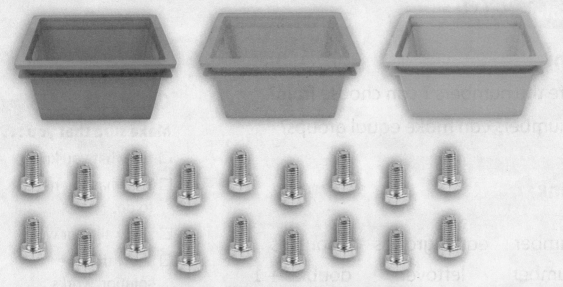

How many bolts can Beau put in each box?

▶ **Solve It** **Show one way that Beau can put the bolts in the boxes.**

- Draw a picture.
- Tell how many bolts to put in each box.
- Explain why your answer works.

▶ **Reflect**

Use Mathematical Practices Talk about this question with a partner.

- **Make Sense of Problems** How did you decide how many bolts to put in each box?

©Curriculum Associates, LLC   Copying is not permitted.

Science Project

Beau has 17 jars. He needs an even number of jars for a science project. He will put the rest of the jars on a shelf.

How many jars could Beau use for the science project?

How many will be left to put on the shelf?

▶ **Solve It** **Tell how many jars Beau could use and how many will be left to put on the shelf.**

- Draw a picture.
- Circle an even number of jars Beau can use.
- Find the number of jars Beau will put on the shelf.
- Show that the total number of jars is 17.

▶ # Reflect

Use Mathematical Practices Talk about this question with a partner.

- **Check Your Answer** What did you do to check that your answer makes sense?

Solve the problems.

1 Mason put his toy cars in equal rows.

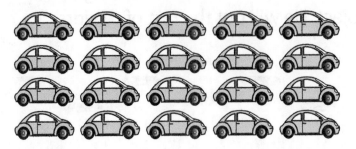

Circle *Yes* or *No* to tell if the equation can be used to find the total number of cars.

a. $4 + 5 + 4 + 5 = ?$ Yes   No

b. $5 + 5 + 5 + 5 + 5 = ?$ Yes   No

c. $4 + 4 + 4 + 4 + 4 = ?$ Yes   No

d. $5 + 5 + 5 + 5 = ?$ Yes   No

2 Lynda scored 9 goals this season. Becca scored 3 fewer goals than Lynda. Which equation can be used to find the number of goals Becca scored? Circle all the correct answers.

A $9 - 3 = 6$

B $12 - 3 = 9$

C $3 + 6 = 9$

D $9 + 3 = 12$

©Curriculum Associates, LLC   Copying is not permitted.

3 Fill in the boxes to show two ways you can find 8 + 6.

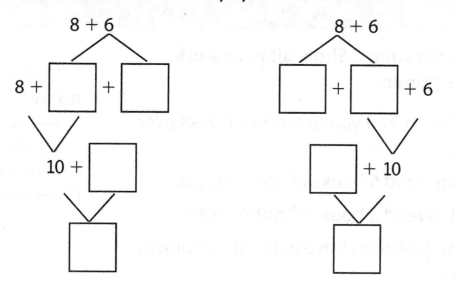

8 + 6

8 + □ + □

10 + □

□

8 + 6

□ + □ + 6

□ + 10

□

4 Write each number in the correct box below.

12   13   15   18

Odd Numbers	Even Numbers

5 Write a word problem that can be solved using this bar model. Then solve your word problem.

7	
?	2

_____

_____

_____

Performance Task

Answer the questions. Show all your work on separate paper.

Your school has asked you to read 20 books over the summer.

- You need to read 6 books about animals.
- You need to read 3 books about people.
- The rest of the books have to be about places or hobbies.
- You have to read at least 1 book about places and 1 book about hobbies.

Make a plan about the books that you will read over the summer.

- Tell how many books about places you will read.
- Tell how many books about hobbies you will read.
- Explain why your numbers work.

Checklist
Did You . . .
☐ add or subtract correctly?
☐ check your answers?
☐ explain your answers?

Reflect

Make an Argument How did you check to see that your numbers work?

©Curriculum Associates, LLC Copying is not permitted.

Unit 2
Number and Operations in Base Ten

Real-World Connection Have you ever counted like this: 10, 20, 30, 40, 50, . . . ? Skip counting by 10s is a fast and easy way to count to 100. You can skip count by 100s too: 100, 200, 300, 400, and so on. Skip counting by 10s and 100s will help you add and subtract two-digit and three-digit numbers.

In This Unit You will learn many ways to add and subtract two-digit and three-digit numbers. You will also learn to add more than 2 two-digit numbers at once!

> Let's learn about adding and subtracting with two-digit and three-digit numbers.

✔ Self Check

Before starting this unit, check off the skills you know below.

I can:	Before this unit	After this unit
add two-digit numbers.	☐	☐
add tens and add ones.	☐	☐
subtract two-digit numbers.	☐	☐
regroup a ten.	☐	☐
solve a one-step word problem by adding or subtracting two-digit numbers.	☐	☐
read and write three-digit numbers.	☐	☐
compare three-digit numbers.	☐	☐
add three-digit numbers.	☐	☐
subtract three-digit numbers.	☐	☐
add more than 2 two-digit numbers.	☐	☐

©Curriculum Associates, LLC   Copying is not permitted.

🄖 Use What You Know

You know how to add one-digit numbers.

One day, Jack found 27 cans to recycle. The next day, he found 15 cans to recycle. How many cans did Jack find altogether?

a. Circle groups of ten in the picture of 27 cans.

There are _____ tens and _____ ones in 27.

b. Circle groups of ten in the picture of 15 cans.

There is _____ ten and _____ ones in 15.

c. How many tens are there in all? _____ tens

d. How many ones are there in all? _____ ones

12 ones = _____ ten and _____ ones

e. How many cans did Jack find? Show your work.

_____

_____

©Curriculum Associates, LLC   Copying is not permitted.

You can add two-digit numbers in many ways.

Here are some ways to find $27 + 15$.

Use base-ten blocks.

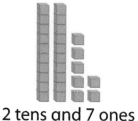 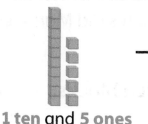 →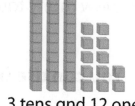

2 tens and 7 ones   **1 ten** and **5 ones**   3 tens and 12 ones

Go to the next ten.
$27 + 3 = 30$
$30 + 10 = 40$
$40 + 2 = 42$

Add tens, then ones.
$20 + 7$
$10 + 5$
$\overline{30 + 12} = 42$

▶ **Reflect** **Work with a partner.**

1 **Talk About It** Show two ways to add 49 and 26.

49   26

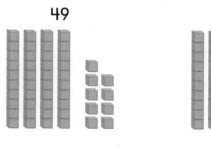

Write About It _____

_____

_____

©Curriculum Associates, LLC   Copying is not permitted.

Learn About **Different Ways to Show Addition**

Read the problem. Then you will explore different ways to show addition.

> Before lunch, Maria read for 38 minutes. After lunch, she read for 45 minutes. How many total minutes did Maria read?

▶ **Picture It** **You can use base-ten blocks.**

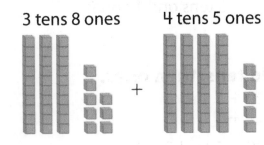

3 tens 8 ones   4 tens 5 ones   7 tens 13 ones

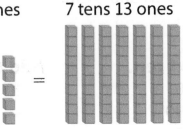

▶ **Model It** **You can add tens and add ones.**

$$38 = 30 + 8$$
$$45 = \underline{40 + 5}$$
$$70 + 13$$

▶ **Model It** **You can go to the next ten.**

$$38 + \mathbf{2} = 40$$

$$40 + \mathbf{40} = 80$$

$$80 + \mathbf{3} = ?$$

      ©Curriculum Associates, LLC   Copying is not permitted.

Connect It Add tens and ones.

2 Look at *Picture It* on the previous page.
What is the total number of tens and ones?

_____ tens + _____ ones

3 How many tens and ones are in 13?

13 = _____ ten and _____ ones, or _____ + 3

4 Add both tens. Then add the ones.

$70 + 10 + 3 =$ _____ + _____

$=$ _____

5 **Talk About It** Explain how you would add 38 and 45.

Write About It _____

_____

_____

_____

Try It Try another problem.

6 Mr. Dane has 17 pens and 13 pencils. How many pens
and pencils does he have in all? Show your work.

_____

_____

Learn About ▸ **More Ways to Show Addition**

Read the problem. Then you will explore different ways to show addition.

There are 48 students on Bus A and 43 students on Bus B. How many students are on both buses?

▸ **Picture It** **You can use a quick drawing.**

Show each number with a quick drawing.

It is easier to add when one number has no ones.
So, make a ten.

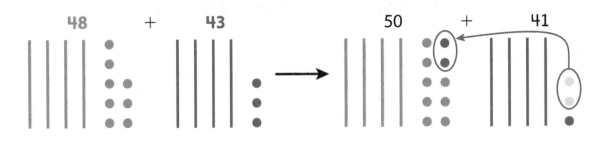

▸ **Model It** **You can use an open number line.**

Start with **48**. Add **2** to go to the next ten. To add **40**, count on by tens from 50: 60, 70, 80, 90. Then add **1** more.

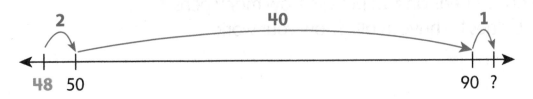

©Curriculum Associates, LLC Copying is not permitted.

▶ **Connect It** **Make a ten to add.**

Look at *Picture It* on the previous page.

7 Why do you add 2 to 48? _____

8 What does the drawing show? Fill in the blanks.

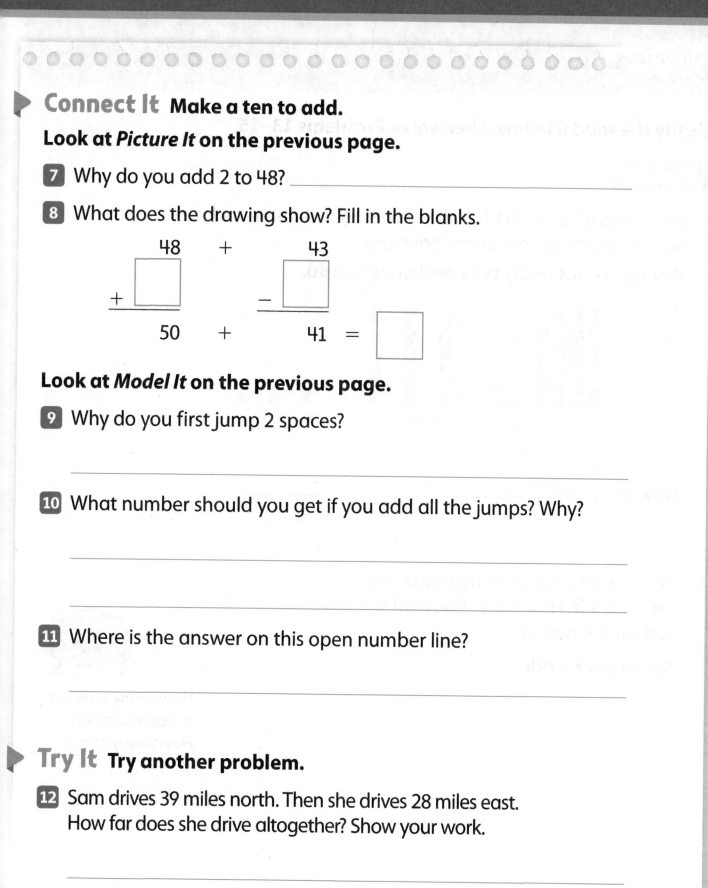

```
   48    +    43
 +[   ]    -[   ]
 ─────    ─────
   50    +    41    =  [   ]
```

Look at *Model It* on the previous page.

9 Why do you first jump 2 spaces?

_____

10 What number should you get if you add all the jumps? Why?

_____

_____

11 Where is the answer on this open number line?

_____

▶ **Try It** **Try another problem.**

12 Sam drives 39 miles north. Then she drives 28 miles east.
How far does she drive altogether? Show your work.

_____

_____

Practice **Adding Two-Digit Numbers**

Study the model below. Then solve Problems 13–15.

Example

Lucas had 47 rocks in his collection. He got 34 more rocks. How many rocks does Lucas have now?

You can count on by tens and ones to add.

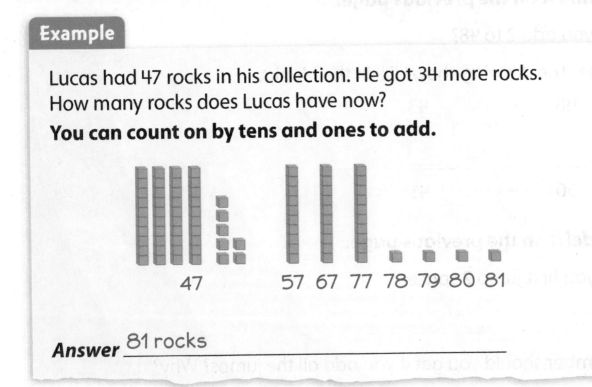

47   57 67 77 78 79 80 81

Answer _81 rocks_

---

13 Bailey sold 12 flags at a parade. She has 14 flags left. How many flags did she have before the parade?

Show your work.

How many tens are in each number? How many ones?

Answer _____

    ©Curriculum Associates, LLC   Copying is not permitted.

14 Kory used 47 blocks to build a tower. Then he used 28 more blocks to make it bigger. How many blocks did Kory use altogether?

Show your work.

What can you add to 47 to get to the next ten?

Answer _____

---

15 Jenny got 53 points in her first card game.
She got 38 points in her second game.
What is the total number of points Jenny got?

A 81

B 93

C 91

D 83

Does it matter which number you start with?

Brady chose **A** as the answer. This answer is wrong.
How did Brady get his answer?

_____

_____

_____

©Curriculum Associates, LLC   Copying is not permitted.

Practice ▶ **Adding Two-Digit Numbers**

Solve the problems.

1 Which addition problem shows a way to add 78 and 16? Circle all the correct answers.

A $70 + 8 + 10 + 6$

B $70 + 10 + 8 + 6$

C $80 + 14$

D $70 + 8 + 6$

2 Jo did 36 sit-ups. Then she did 27 more. How many sit-ups did Jo do in all? Circle the correct answer.

A 73

B 63

C 53

D 9

3 Tell if the equation shows how to find $24 + 9$. Circle *Yes* or *No* for each problem.

a. $20 + 4 + 9 = 33$ Yes   No

b. $2 + 4 + 9 = 15$ Yes   No

c. $20 + 40 + 9 = 69$ Yes   No

d. $20 + 10 + 3 = 33$ Yes   No

©Curriculum Associates, LLC   Copying is not permitted.

4 Each morning, Seth runs 1 more minute than the day before. Yesterday, he ran for 14 minutes. How many total minutes did he run yesterday and today? Circle the correct answer.

A 14   **C** 27

B 15   **D** 29

5 Ms. Ames shows her students the problem at the right. What did she do? Explain. Then show how to solve the problem a different way.

$$\begin{array}{r} 25 \\ +\ 59 \\ \hline 14 \\ +\ 70 \\ \hline 84 \end{array}$$

_____

_____

6 Find 47 + 24 the way Ms. Ames did in Problem 5. Then use a different way. What do you notice?

_____

_____

✓ **Self Check**   **Now you can add two-digit numbers. Fill this in on the progress chart on page 59.**

Subtract Two-Digit Numbers

🔄 Use What You Know

You know how to count tens and ones.

There are 34 art projects in a contest.
There are 9 paintings.
The rest are drawings.
How many art projects are drawings?

a. How many tens and ones are in 34?

_____ tens and _____ ones

b. Solve 34 − 9 to find the number of drawings.

How many ones do you need to subtract? _____

c. Are there enough ones in 34 to subtract? _____

Explain. _____

_____

d. Look at the model at the right.

How many tens blocks are there? _____ tens

How many ones blocks are there? _____ ones

e. Now take away 9 ones. How many tens and ones

are left? _____ tens and _____ ones

f. How many art projects are drawings? _____

©Curriculum Associates, LLC   Copying is not permitted.

Here are two ways to find 34 − 9.

Start at 9 and add up to 34.

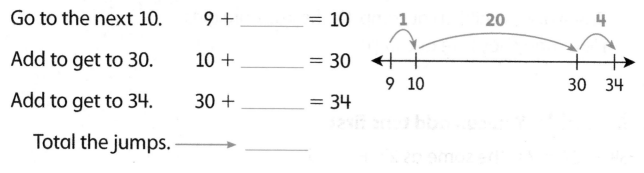

Go to the next 10.   9 + _____ = 10

Add to get to 30.   10 + _____ = 30

Add to get to 34.   30 + _____ = 34

Total the jumps. ⟶ _____

9 + _____ = 34, so 34 − 9 = _____

Subtract to make a ten.

34 has 4 ones, so subtract 4 first. Then subtract 5.

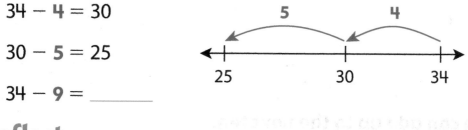

34 − 4 = 30

30 − 5 = 25

34 − 9 = _____

▶ Reflect

1 Talk About It How can you subtract 8 from 46? Explain one way.

Write About It _____

_____

_____

Learn About Subtracting by Adding Up

Read the problem. Then you will add up to subtract two-digit numbers.

There are 54 children at camp. Of these, 27 are girls.
How many boys are at camp?

▶ **Model It** **You can add tens first.**

$54 - 27 = ?$ is the same as $27 + ? = 54$.

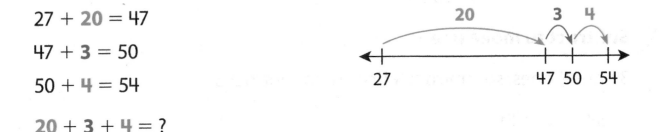

$27 + 20 = 47$

$47 + 3 = 50$

$50 + 4 = 54$

$20 + 3 + 4 = ?$

▶ **Model It** **You can add up to the next ten.**

Find $54 - 27$.

Start with 27 and add 3.
Then add 20 to get to 50.
Finally, add 4 to get to 54.

You can count up
by 10s to add 20.
Think: 40, 50.

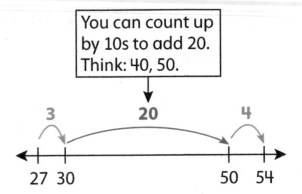

$27 + 3 = 30$

$30 + 20 = 50$

$50 + 4 = 54$

$3 + 20 + 4 = ?$

 ©Curriculum Associates, LLC Copying is not permitted.

▶ Connect It Understand adding up.

Look at the first *Model It*.

2 What number do you start with? _____

What number do you stop at? _____

Look at the second *Model It*.

3 Why do you add 3 first? _____

_____

4 What is 54 − 27? How did you get your answer?

_____

_____

5 **Talk About It** How are the two models on the previous page alike? How are they different?

Write About It _____

_____

_____

▶ Try It Try another problem.

6 Subtract 16 from 30 by adding up. Show your work.

_____

Learn About ▶ Subtracting by Regrouping

Read the problem. Then you will subtract in different ways.

> Ming had 42 toy animals. She gave 15 toy animals to her friends. How many toy animals does Ming have left?

▶ **Model It** **You can regroup a ten first and then subtract.**

Find $42 - 15$.

Step 1: Make 10 ones with 1 ten in 42.

$42 = 3$ tens and 12 ones

Step 2: Subtract.

$$\begin{array}{r} 3 \text{ tens and } 12 \text{ ones} \\ - 1 \text{ ten and } 5 \text{ ones} \\ \hline \end{array}$$

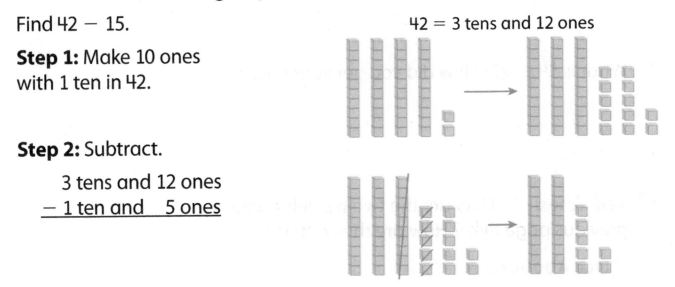

▶ **Model It** **You can subtract tens first.**

Find $42 - 15$.

Step 1: $15 = 1$ ten and 5 ones.

Take away 1 ten.

$$42 - 10 = 32$$

Step 2: Make 10 ones with 1 ten. Then take away 5 ones.

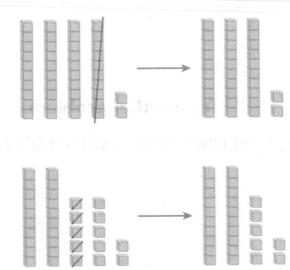

©Curriculum Associates, LLC   Copying is not permitted.

Connect It Understand ways to subtract.

Look at the first *Model It* on the previous page.

7 Why do you make 10 ones with 1 ten in 42?

_____

8 How many tens and ones are left after you

subtract in Step 2? _____ tens and _____ ones

Look at the second *Model It* on the previous page.

9 How many tens and ones are left after you

subtract 1 ten? _____ tens and _____ ones

10 How many tens and ones are left after you

subtract 5 ones? _____ tens and _____ ones

11 How many toy animals does Ming have left? _____

12 **Talk About It** How is Step 1 in the first *Model It*
different from Step 1 in the second *Model It*?
Does it matter what you do first?

Write About It _____

_____

_____

Try It Try another problem.

13 Subtract 63 from 82 by taking away tens and ones.
Show your work.

_____

Practice ▶ **Subtracting Two-Digit Numbers**

Study the model below. Then solve Problems 14–16.

Example

Joe has 52 cards. He puts 28 cards in one pile and the rest in a second pile. How many cards are in the second pile? Find 52 − 28.

You can show your work on an open number line.

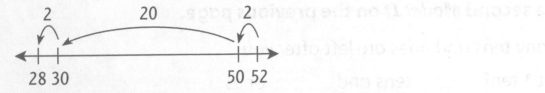

Jump down 2 + 20 + 2, or 24, to get to 28.
So, 52 − 28 = 24.

Answer _24 cards_____

---

14 At the farm, there are 25 fruit trees. Of these, 18 are apple trees. The rest are pear trees. How many pear trees are there? Find 25 − 18.

Show your work.

If you add up, what number do you start with?

Answer _____

©Curriculum Associates, LLC   Copying is not permitted.

15 There are 71 students on two buses. One bus has 38 students. How many are on the other bus? Find 71 − 38.

Show your work.

What number can you subtract if you subtract tens first?

Answer _____

---

16 Pedro does 27 jumping jacks. Ray does 8 fewer jumping jacks than Pedro. How many jumping jacks does Ray do? Find 27 − 8.

A 9

B 19

C 20

D 35

How many do you take away from 27 to make a ten?

Mia chose **D** as the answer. This answer is wrong. How did Mia get her answer?

_____

_____

_____

©Curriculum Associates, LLC   Copying is not permitted.

Practice ▶ **Subtracting Two-Digit Numbers**

Solve the problems.

1 How can you find 35 − 17? Circle all the
   correct answers.

   A 35 − 5 = 30 and 30 − 2 = 28

   B 35 − 10 = 25 and 25 − 7 = 18

   C 17 + 10 = 27 and 27 + 7 = 34

   D 17 + 3 = 20 and 20 + 15 = 35

2 Jamie drew this model to solve a problem. Which
   problem did she solve? Circle the correct answer.

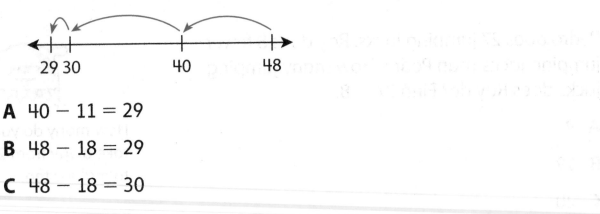

   A 40 − 11 = 29

   B 48 − 18 = 29

   C 48 − 18 = 30

   D 48 − 19 = 29

3 Don had 22 shells. He gave 5 to his brother.
   How many shells does Don have now?
   Find 22 − 5. Circle the correct answer.

   A 7

   B 12

   C 17

   D 29

 ©Curriculum Associates, LLC   Copying is not permitted.

4 Circle *Yes* or *No* to tell if you can use the method to find 56 − 17.

a. 56 − 6 = 50 and
   50 − 1 = 49   Yes   No

b. 56 − 10 = 46 and
   46 − 7 = 39   Yes   No

c. 17 + 3 = 20 and
   20 + 36 = 56   Yes   No

d.   4 tens and 16 ones
    − 1 ten and 7 ones   Yes   No
      3 tens and 9 ones

5 Greg subtracted 44 from 73. He forgot the last step.
Write the last step and the answer in the boxes.
Explain how Greg subtracted.

_____

_____

_____

$$\begin{array}{r} 73 \\ -\ 40 \\ \hline 33 \\ -\ 3 \\ \hline 30 \\ -\ \boxed{} \\ \hline \boxed{} \end{array}$$

6 Show another way to subtract 44 from 73.
Make sure it is different from what you did
in Problem 5.

✓ **Self Check** **Now you can subtract two-digit numbers.**
Fill this in on the progress chart on page 59.

Solve One-Step Word Problems with Two-Digit Numbers

Ⓖ Use What You Know

Review solving one-step word problems.

Mr. Soto's students can trade 75 box tops for school supplies. They have 49 box tops. How many more do they need to get to 75?

a. What is the total number of box tops the class can trade? Write this number in the model.

b. How many box tops does the class start with? Write this number in the model.

	?

c. Use the model. Fill in the blanks below to write an equation.

_____ + ? = _____

d. Find the missing number. Show your work.

e. How many more box tops does the class need? _____

▷▷ Find Out More

You can use models for *start, change,* and *total* problems.

Here is one way to think of the problem on the previous page.

- **Start** with a number. (49 box tops)

- **Change** happens. (Collect more box tops.)

- Get a **total**. (75 box tops)

You can use any of these models to show the problem.

You can use any of these equations to solve the problem.

Addition	**Subtraction**
$49 + ? = 75$	$75 - 49 = ?$
$? + 49 = 75$	$75 - ? = 49$

▶ Reflect **Work with a partner.**

1 **Talk About It** Look at the equations above. The ⬚? and numbers are in different places. Why is the answer to all the equations 26?

Write About It _____

_____

_____

Learn About ▶ **Ways to Model Word Problems**

Read the problem. Then you will use addition and subtraction equations to model the problem.

Todd plays a game. The table shows his points.

Level 1	?
Level 2	16 points
Total	55 points

How many points did Todd get in Level 1?

▶ **Picture It** **You can draw a bar model.**

55	
?	16

▶ **Model It** **You can use an addition equation.**

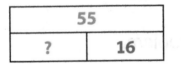

Level 1 Score + Level 2 Score = Total Score

? + 16 = 55

▶ **Model It** **You can use a subtraction equation.**

Total Score − Level 2 Score = Level 1 Score

55 − 16 = ?

©Curriculum Associates, LLC   Copying is not permitted.

Connect It Understand addition and subtraction equations.

2 Look at *Picture It*. What does the ⬚? mean?

_____

3 Look at the second *Model It*. Write a different subtraction equation that you could use to solve the problem.

_____ − _____ = _____

4 Solve the problem from the previous page. Show your work on the open number line. Then write your answer.

⟵─────────────────────⟶

_____

5 **Talk About It** How did you make your number line in Problem 4? What is another way to find the answer?

Write About It _____

_____

_____

▶ Try It Try another problem.

6 Matt had 72 sports cards. Then he got more cards. Now he has 90 cards. How many more cards did Matt get? Show your work.

_____

Learn About   **More Ways to Model Word Problems**

Read the problem. Then you will use words and numbers to model the problem.

Some books were on a shelf. Students took 24 books from the shelf. Then there were 38 books on the shelf. How many books were on the shelf to begin with?

▶ **Model It** **You can show the problem with words.**

You can model the problem with words.

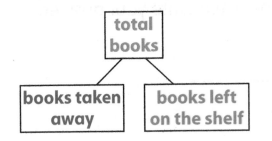

▶ **Model It** **You can show the problem with numbers.**

You can model the problem with numbers.

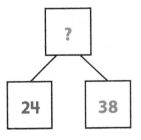

©Curriculum Associates, LLC   Copying is not permitted.

Connect It Write an equation to solve the problem.

7 Look at the second *Model It*. Write an addition equation and a subtraction equation for the problem.

_____ = _____ + _____   _____ − _____ = _____

8 Write a different addition equation that you could use to solve the problem.

_____ + _____ = _____

9 What was the total number of books on the shelf to begin with? Show your work.

_____

_____

10 **Talk About It** How did your partner solve the problem?

Write About It _____

_____

_____

Try It Try another problem.

11 Students are helping clean the park. At noon, 33 students went home. There are 48 students left. How many students started? Show your work.

_____

_____

Practice ▶ Modeling and Solving Word Problems

Study the model below. Then solve Problems 12–14.

Example

Keesha's math test score is 95. John's score is 13 points less than Keesha's score. What is John's score?

You can show your work on an open number line.

Keesha's score − 13 = John's score   95 − 13 = ?

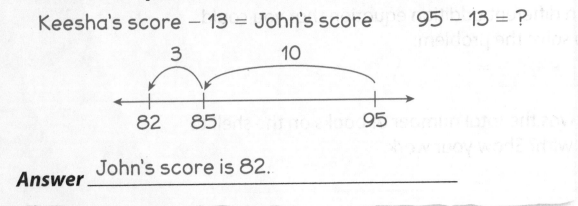

Answer _John's score is 82._

---

12 There were 22 people on a train. More people got on at the next stop. Now there are 51 people on the train. How many people got on at the stop?

Show your work.

Can you make a model to help you think about the problem?

Answer _____

©Curriculum Associates, LLC   Copying is not permitted.

13 There are 27 small dogs and 26 big dogs in the pet show. How many dogs are in the pet show?

Show your work.

Do you add or subtract to solve the problem?

Answer _____

14 Liz makes 42 jumps with a jump rope. Tia makes 17 fewer jumps. How many jumps does Tia make?

A 15

B 22

C 25

D 59

Which girl makes more jumps?

Ramin chose **D** as the answer. This answer is wrong. How did Ramin get his answer?

_____

_____

_____

Practice ▶ Modeling and Solving Word Problems

Solve the problems.

1 Ty is 47 inches tall. Meg is 56 inches tall.
How much taller is Meg?

Which equation can you use to solve this problem?
Circle all the correct answers.

A $56 + ? = 47$

B $47 + ? = 56$

C $56 = 47 + ?$

D $56 - ? = 47$

2 A beagle weighs 26 pounds. A pug weighs
8 pounds less than the beagle. How many pounds
does the pug weigh? Circle the correct answer.

A 34

B 20

C 18

D 13

3 Sara has 52 pens. She puts them into two cups.
Complete each equation to show some of the ways
Sara could put her pens into the two cups.

$26 +$ _____ $= 52$ _____ $+ 27 = 52$

_____ $+ 23 = 52$ $34 +$ _____ $= 52$

4 There are 32 students in a school play. There are 17 girls. The rest are boys. How many boys are in the play? Circle the correct answer.

A 49

B 15

C 13

D 12

5 There are 64 balls and 58 bats in the gym. How many more balls are there than bats?

Circle *Yes* or *No* to tell if each equation can be used to solve the problem.

a. $58 + ? = 64$ Yes   No

b. $64 - 58 = ?$ Yes   No

c. $64 + 58 = ?$ Yes   No

d. $64 - ? = 58$ Yes   No

6 Write a one-step word problem that uses addition or subtraction with two-digit numbers. Then solve the problem.

_____

_____

✓ **Self Check** **Now you can solve problems using two-digit numbers. Fill this in on the progress chart on page 59.**

💭 Think It Through

What is one hundred?

You can count to one hundred. After 99 is **100**.

1	2	3	4	5	6	7	8	9	10
11	12	13	14	15	16	17	18	19	20
21	22	23	24	25	26	27	28	29	30
31	32	33	34	35	36	37	38	39	40
41	42	43	44	45	46	47	48	49	50
51	52	53	54	55	56	57	58	59	60
61	62	63	64	65	66	67	68	69	70
71	72	73	74	75	76	77	78	79	80
81	82	83	84	85	86	87	88	89	90
91	92	93	94	95	96	97	98	99	**100**

Think One hundred is 100 ones. One hundred is 10 tens.

100 = 100 ones

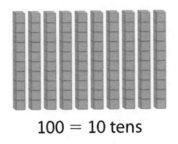

100 = 10 tens

✏️ Circle groups of 10 ones in 100.

©Curriculum Associates, LLC   Copying is not permitted.

Think One hundred can be shown as hundreds, tens, or ones.

Fill in the blanks.

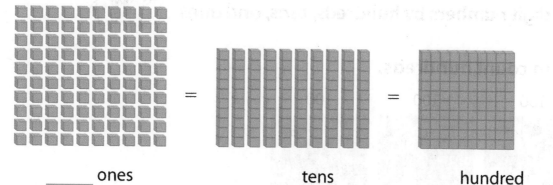

_____ ones = _____ tens = _____ hundred

Ways to Show 100			
Hundreds	**Tens**	**Ones**	
0	0	100	0 hundreds + 0 tens + 100 ones
0	10	0	0 hundreds + 10 tens + 0 ones
1	0	0	1 hundred + 0 tens + 0 ones

100
↑
hundreds place

A three-digit number has a hundreds place. It tells how many hundreds there are in a number.

▶ Reflect Work with a partner.

1 **Talk About It** Think about 200. How many hundreds does 200 have? How many tens? How many ones?

Write About It _____

_____

_____

©Curriculum Associates, LLC   Copying is not permitted.

| Think About | **Hundreds, Tens, and Ones** |

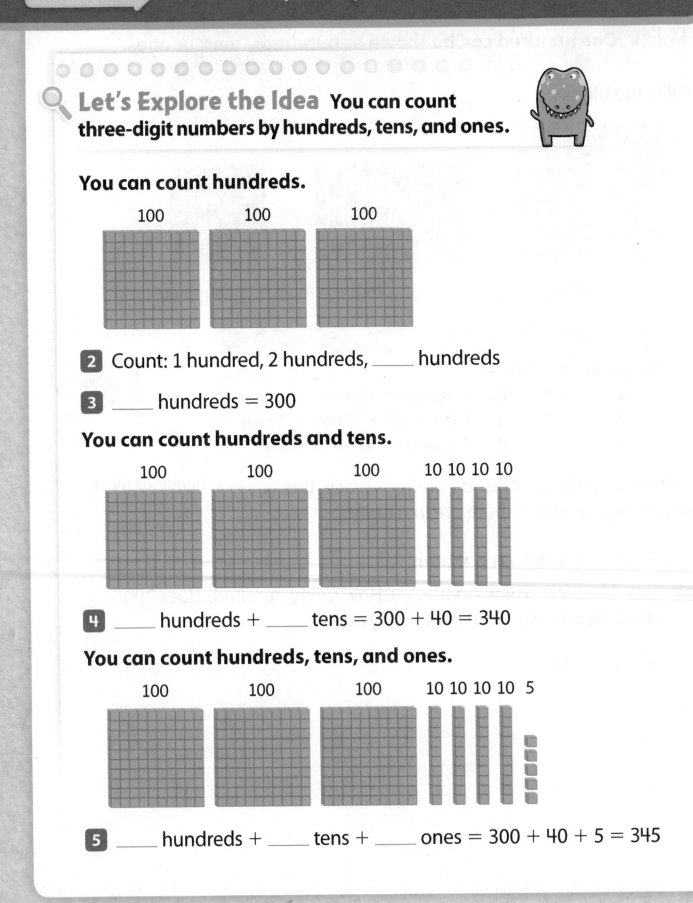

🔍 **Let's Explore the Idea** **You can count three-digit numbers by hundreds, tens, and ones.**

You can count hundreds.

100   100   100

2 Count: 1 hundred, 2 hundreds, _____ hundreds

3 _____ hundreds = 300

You can count hundreds and tens.

100   100   100   10 10 10 10

4 _____ hundreds + _____ tens = 300 + 40 = 340

You can count hundreds, tens, and ones.

100   100   100   10 10 10 10 5

5 _____ hundreds + _____ tens + _____ ones = 300 + 40 + 5 = 345

©Curriculum Associates, LLC   Copying is not permitted.

Let's Talk About It
Work with a partner.

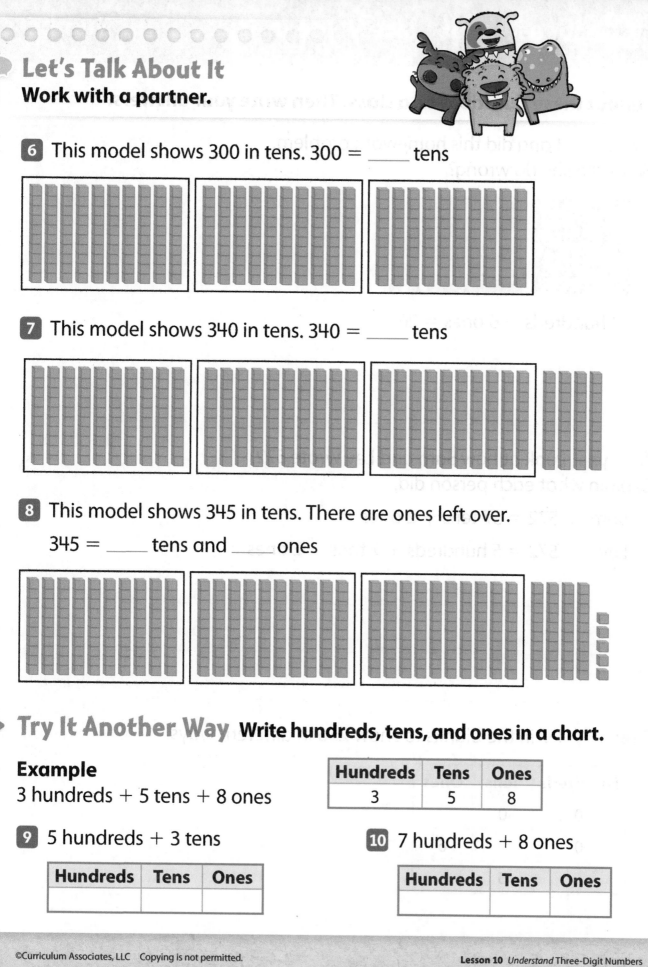

6 This model shows 300 in tens. 300 = _____ tens

7 This model shows 340 in tens. 340 = _____ tens

8 This model shows 345 in tens. There are ones left over.

345 = _____ tens and _____ ones

Try It Another Way Write hundreds, tens, and ones in a chart.

Example
3 hundreds + 5 tens + 8 ones

Hundreds	Tens	Ones
3	5	8

9 5 hundreds + 3 tens

Hundreds	Tens	Ones

10 7 hundreds + 8 ones

Hundreds	Tens	Ones

©Curriculum Associates, LLC   Copying is not permitted.

Talk about these questions as a class. Then write your answers.

11 **Evaluate** Lana did this homework problem. What did she do wrong?

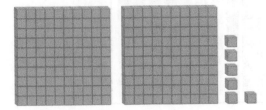

2 hundreds + 6 ones = 26

_____

_____

12 **Analyze** Look at how Sam and Lev wrote 572. Explain what each person did.

Sam   572 = 57 tens + 2 ones

Lev   572 = 5 hundreds + 7 tens + 2 ones

_____

_____

_____

13 **Identify** Fill in the blanks to show 256 in different ways.

Hundreds	Tens	Ones
0	0	
0		6
	5	

©Curriculum Associates, LLC   Copying is not permitted.

Apply   Ideas About Place Value in Three-Digit Numbers

Put It Together   **Use what you have learned to complete this task.**

14   Nate puts his coins in stacks of ten. He has
12 stacks of coins with 4 coins left over.

Part A   Draw a picture to show Nate's coins.

Part B   How many coins does Nate have? Write the
answer in two different ways.

_____

_____

Part C   Nate gets 30 more coins from a friend. Nate says that he
now has 190 coins. Do you agree or disagree? Explain.

_____

_____

_____

_____

Ⓖ Use What You Know

Write three-digit numbers with hundreds, tens, and ones.

Jan buys 2 packs of 100 balloons. She also buys 7 packs of 10 balloons and 5 single balloons. How many balloons does Jan buy?

a. 2 packs of 100 = _____ hundreds

The number of balloons in 2 packs of 100 is _____.

b. 7 packs of 10 = _____ tens

The number of balloons in 7 packs of ten is _____.

c. 5 single balloons = _____ ones

The number of single balloons is _____.

d. Complete the equation to find the total number of balloons.

_____ + _____ + _____ = _____
  100s   10s   1s

©Curriculum Associates, LLC   Copying is not permitted.

Find Out More

The **digits** 0, 1, 2, 3, 4, 5, 6, 7, 8, and 9 make up all numbers. The digit's place in a number tells its value.

The same digit can have different values.
Look at the value of each 4 in this number.

Hundreds	Tens	Ones
4	4	4
↓	↓	↓
400	40	4

Reflect Work with a partner.

1 **Talk About It** When does the digit 8 have a value of 8? 80? 800? What are some three-digit numbers that show these values?

Write About It ______________________________

____

____

____

____

____

©Curriculum Associates, LLC Copying is not permitted.

Learn About ➤ **Finding the Value of Three-Digit Numbers**

Read the problem. Then you will show hundreds, tens, and ones in different ways.

> Amir plays a board game that uses play money.
> He wins 2 hundreds bills, 1 tens bill, and 3 ones bills.
> What is the total value of the bills Amir wins?

➤ **Picture It** **You can draw a picture to show the problem.**

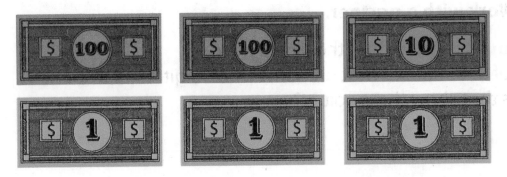

➤ **Picture It** **You can make a quick drawing to show hundreds, tens, and ones.**

➤ **Model It** **You can show hundreds, tens, and ones in a chart.**

Hundreds	Tens	Ones
2	1	3

©Curriculum Associates, LLC   Copying is not permitted.

Connect It Write the number as hundreds, tens, and ones.

2 Look at the models on the previous page.
How many hundreds, tens, and ones are there?

_____ hundreds _____ ten _____ ones

3 What is the value of the hundreds bills? _____ dollars

What is the value of the tens bill? _____ dollars

What is the value of the ones bills? _____ dollars

4 Write an equation to find the total value of all the bills.

_____ + _____ + _____ = _____ dollars

5 **Talk About It** Amir wins 2 more tens bills. How would you write the new total value of Amir's play money? Explain how you found your answer.

Write About It _____

_____

_____

_____

Try It Try another problem.

6 What is another way to show each number? Draw lines to connect each number to another way to write the number.

392   329   239

300 + 20 + 9   200 + 30 + 9   300 + 90 + 2

Practice ▶ **Reading and Writing Three-Digit Numbers**

Study the model below. Then solve Problems 7–9.

Example

Mrs. Cole wrote this number on a check.

five hundred ninety-four

What is this number?

You can show your work in a chart.

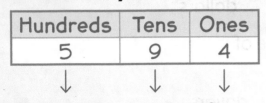

Hundreds	Tens	Ones
5	9	4

↓   ↓   ↓

five hundred ninety-four

Answer ___The number is 594.___

---

7 Pat wrote these clues about his secret number.

- The hundreds digit is 1 more than 8.
- The tens digit has a value of 40.
- The number has 2 ones.

What is the secret number?

Show your work.

How many digits are in the number?

Answer _____

 ©Curriculum Associates, LLC   Copying is not permitted.

8 Jim is playing a board game. This is Jim's play money. Write the amount in two different ways.

What is the value of each kind of bill in the problem?

_____ dollars + _____ dollars + _____ dollars

_____ dollars

9 Which number is the same as 700 + 6?

A 76

B 607

C 706

D 760

How many tens does the number have?

Zoey chose **A** as the answer. This answer is wrong. How did Zoey get her answer?

_____

_____

_____

Practice ▶ **Reading and Writing Three-Digit Numbers**

Solve the problems.

1 What is another way to show 2 hundreds and 5 ones? Circle all the correct answers.

A 200 + 5

B 25

C 200 + 50

D 205

2 What does the model show? Fill in the table and the blanks.

Hundreds	Tens	Ones

Value: _____ + _____ + _____

Total: _____

3 A bear at the zoo weighs 360 pounds. What is true about this number? Circle all the correct answers.

A It is 300 + 6.

B It equals 36 tens.

C It is 300 + 60.

D It has 3 hundreds and 6 tens.

©Curriculum Associates, LLC Copying is not permitted.

4 Here are clues about a number.

- The number has 7 hundreds.

- The tens digit has a value of 30.

- The ones digit is less than any other digit in the number.

What could the number be? Explain.

_____

_____

_____

5 Write the value of each digit in the two numbers.

275	527
_____ + _____ + _____	_____ + _____ + _____

6 Look at Problem 5. Why do the 2, 5, and 7 have a different value in each number? Explain.

_____

_____

✔ Self Check **Now you can write three-digit numbers. Fill this in on the progress chart on page 59.**

Lesson 12 😾 Introduction
Compare Three-Digit Numbers

◔ Use What You Know

Compare hundreds and tens.

Kim and Jon tossed beanbags at a target. What is the greatest number each person can make using the digits they landed on? Whose number has more hundreds?

a. What is the greatest number Kim can make? Why?

_____

_____

b. One of Jon's beanbags did not land on the board, so he can only use two numbers. What is the greatest number Jon can make? Why?

_____

_____

c. How many hundreds, tens, and ones are in each number?

Kim's number: _____ hundreds + _____ tens + _____ one

Jon's number: _____ hundreds + _____ tens + _____ ones

d. Compare the numbers. Which has more hundreds?

_____

©Curriculum Associates, LLC Copying is not permitted.

When you compare numbers, always start with the greatest place value. Compare the digits in each place.

	Hundreds	Tens	Ones
Jon	0	9	7
Kim	4	2	1

4 hundreds is greater than 0 hundreds.

The number with more hundreds is greater. So 421 is greater than 97.

You can use the symbols $<$, $>$, and $=$ to compare numbers.

Think of the $<$ and $>$ as a hungry alligator's mouth that is always open to eat the greater number.

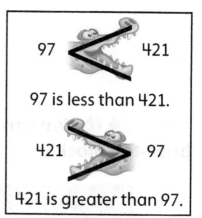

97 $<$ 421

97 is less than 421.

421 $>$ 97

421 is greater than 97.

▶ **Reflect** **Work with a partner.**

1 **Talk About It** Why is a three-digit number always greater than a two-digit number?

Write About It _____

_____

_____

Learn About ▶ **Ways to Compare Three-Digit Numbers**

Read the problem. Then you will compare two three-digit numbers.

There is a contest at the school fair. Students guess how many jelly beans are in a jar. Bart guesses 352 and Diego guesses 328. Which guess is the lesser number?

▶ **Picture It** **You can model the numbers with base-ten blocks.**

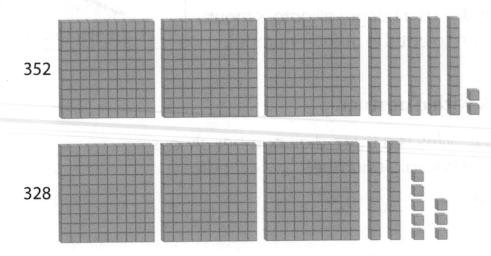

352

328

▶ **Model It** **You can write the numbers as hundreds, tens, and ones.**

352 = 3 hundreds + 5 tens + 2 ones

328 = 3 hundreds + 2 tens + 8 ones

©Curriculum Associates, LLC Copying is not permitted.

Connect It Understand how to compare numbers.

2 Look at the models on the previous page. Can you use the numbers in the hundreds place to decide which number is greater? Why or why not?

_____

3 Now compare the tens. Which number has more tens?

_____

4 Complete the number sentence to compare 352 and 328.

_____ < _____

5 **Talk About It** Bart says 2 < 8, so 352 < 328. Is this correct? Explain.

Write About It _____

_____

_____

Try It Try another problem.

6 Write a number sentence to compare 761 and 716. Explain why the number sentence is true.

_____

_____

_____

Learn About ▶ **More Ways to Compare Three-Digit Numbers**

Read the problem. Then you will compare in different ways.

These two paintings are in the school art contest.
Which painting has more votes?

Painting A: 467 Votes

Painting B: 463 Votes

▶ **Picture It** **You can show the numbers in a quick drawing.**

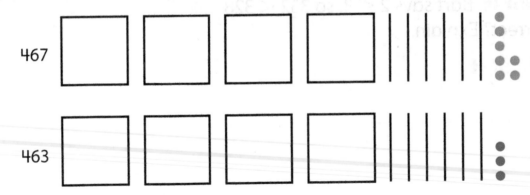

▶ **Model It** **You can model the numbers in a chart.**

Hundreds	Tens	Ones
4	6	7
4	6	3

©Curriculum Associates, LLC Copying is not permitted.

Connect It Compare hundreds, tens, and ones.

7 Look at the models on the previous page. Compare the hundreds and tens. What do you notice?

_____

8 Which place do you need to look at to compare the numbers? Why?

_____

_____

9 Use the numbers 467 and 463 to complete each number sentence.

_____ > _____   _____ < _____

10 Why can you write two different number sentences to compare 467 and 463?

_____

_____

11 Which painting has more votes? How do you know?

_____

Try It Try another problem.

12 Write > or < in each blank.

a. 264 _____ 462   **c.** 954 _____ 950   **e.** 718 _____ 788

b. 372 _____ 379   **d.** 876 _____ 867   **f.** 653 _____ 553

Practice ➤ **Comparing Three-Digit Numbers**

Study the model below. Then solve Problems 13–15.

Example

Yen packs 250 oranges in a box. Gia packs 25 bags of oranges.
She puts 10 oranges in each bag. Who packs more oranges?

Look at how you can show your work.

> 25 bags with 10 in each bag = 25 tens
>
> 25 tens = 250

250 oranges in bags
250 oranges in a box
250 = 250

Answer They each pack 250 oranges. Neither person

packs more than the other.

---

13 Which two players have the greatest scores? Write
the number of hundreds and tens in the table.

Player	Score	Hundreds	Tens
Eden	92		
Sarita	233		
Paul	213		
Chen	236		

Show your work.

Remember to look
at the hundreds
place first.

Answer _____

©Curriculum Associates, LLC   Copying is not permitted.

14 Bella biked 122 miles. Ariel biked 126 miles. Who biked fewer miles?

Show your work.

Are you looking for the lesser or greater number?

Answer _____

---

15 Jill and Iman each write a three-digit number.

Jill's number: 305

Iman's number: 3 hundreds 5 tens

Which number sentence compares their numbers correctly?

What number is the same as 3 hundreds 5 tens?

A 305 < 305

B 305 = 305

C 350 > 305

D 350 < 305

Dan chose **B** as the answer. This answer is wrong. How did Dan get his answer?

_____

_____

Practice ▸ **Comparing Three-Digit Numbers**

Solve the problems.

1 Which comparison is true? Circle all the correct answers.

A 431 > 427

B 540 < 5 hundreds 4 ones

C 727 < 772

D 9 hundreds 6 tens < 906

2 Phil has 248 trading cards. Sean has more trading cards than Phil. How many cards could Sean have? Circle all the correct answers.

A 239

B 245

C 252

D 260

3 Choose *True* or *False* for each comparison.

a. 551 > 539   True   False

b. 924 < 889   True   False

c. 770 = 707   True   False

d. 422 < 425   True   False

©Curriculum Associates, LLC   Copying is not permitted.

4 Write one of the numbers below in each box to make a true comparison.

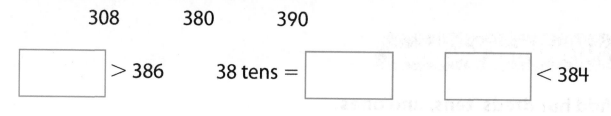

308　　　　380　　　　390

[　　　] > 386　　　38 tens = [　　　]　　　[　　　] < 384

5 Use the digits below to make the greatest three-digit number you can. Explain how you got your answer.

[4]　[1]　[8]

_____

_____

_____

6 Josh wants to use the digits from Problem 5 to make the least number he can. He writes 184. Is this the least number he can make? Explain.

_____

_____

_____

 **Self Check** **Now you can compare three-digit numbers. Fill this in on the progress chart on page 59.**

⟲ Use What You Know

Add hundreds, tens, and ones.

There are 214 fish in the giant tank at an aquarium. There are 131 other sea animals in the tank. How many animals live in the giant tank?

a. How many hundreds, tens, and ones are in each number? Fill in the table.

	Hundreds	Tens	Ones
214			
131			

b. What is the total number of hundreds, tens, and ones in the chart?

_____ hundreds _____ tens _____ ones

c. What is the value of the total number of hundreds, tens, and ones?

_____ + _____ + _____

d. How many animals live in the giant tank?

$214 + 131 =$ _____

©Curriculum Associates, LLC   Copying is not permitted.

There are other ways to find the sum of 214 and 131.

Here are two ways to break apart addends.

214 → 200 + 10 + 4	214 → 2 hundreds + 1 ten + 4 ones
+ 131 → 100 + 30 + 1	+ 131 → 1 hundred + 3 tens + 1 one
345 ← 300 + 40 + 5	345 ← 3 hundreds + 4 tens + 5 ones

You can also show jumps on an open number line.

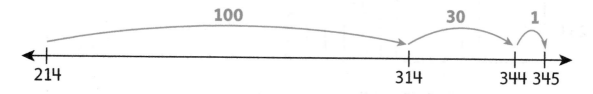

Reflect Work with a partner.

1 **Talk About It** Do you always have to add hundreds, then tens, then ones? Why or why not?

Write About It _____

_____

_____

_____

Learn About ❯ **Adding Hundreds, Tens, and Ones**

Read the problem. Then you will show the addends in different ways.

There are 254 adults and 328 children helping to clean up their city. How many people are helping to clean up the city?

▶ **Picture It** **You can show the numbers in a quick drawing.**

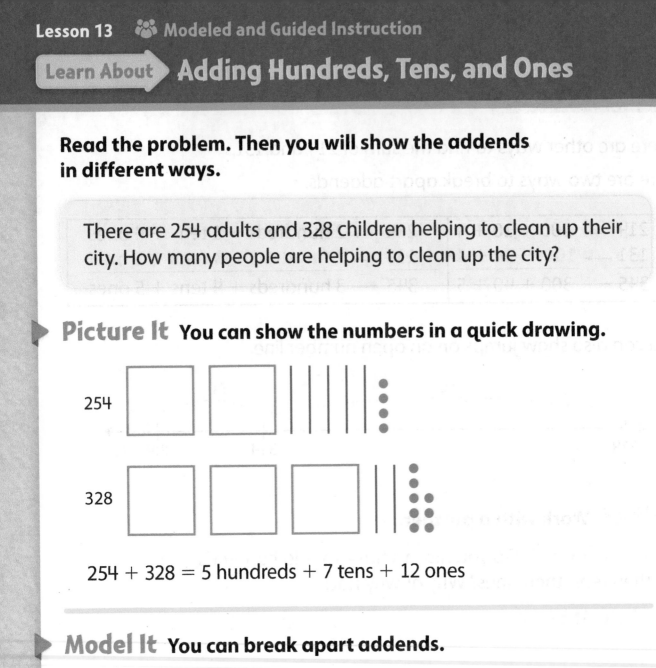

254 + 328 = 5 hundreds + 7 tens + 12 ones

▶ **Model It** **You can break apart addends.**

$$
\begin{array}{r}
254 \rightarrow 200 + 50 + 4 \\
+\,328 \rightarrow 300 + 20 + 8 \\
\hline
500 + 70 + 12
\end{array}
$$

©Curriculum Associates, LLC   Copying is not permitted.

Connect It Make a ten to add.

2 Look at *Picture It*. How do you write 12 ones as tens and ones?

12 ones = _____ ten + _____ ones

3 Look at *Model It*. What is the total number of tens in 70 + 12? Explain.

_____

_____

_____

4 How many people are helping to clean the city? Show how to find the sum.

_____

_____

Try It Try more problems.

Find each sum. Show your work.

5
$$\begin{array}{r} 526 \\ + \ 235 \\ \hline \end{array}$$

6 167 + 426

Learn About ▶ **Adding Three-Digit Numbers**

Read the problem. Then you will model addition in different ways.

> There are 476 rocks and 148 minerals in a museum display. What is the total number of rocks and minerals in the display?

▶ **Model It** **You can show each number as hundreds, tens, and ones.**

$$476 \longrightarrow 4 \text{ hundreds} + 7 \text{ tens} + 6 \text{ ones}$$
$$+ 148 \longrightarrow 1 \text{ hundred} + 4 \text{ tens} + 8 \text{ ones}$$
$$\overline{ \quad 5 \text{ hundreds} + 11 \text{ tens} + 14 \text{ ones}}$$

▶ **Model It** **You can add hundreds, then tens, then ones.**

$$
\begin{array}{r}
476 \\
+ 148 \\
\hline
500 \longrightarrow 400 + 100 \\
110 \longrightarrow 70 + 40 \\
14 \longrightarrow 6 + 8 \\
\end{array}
$$

$$500 + 110 + 14$$

▶ **Model It** **You can add ones, then tens, then hundreds.**

$$
\begin{array}{r}
476 \\
+ 148 \\
\hline
14 \longrightarrow 6 + 8 \\
110 \longrightarrow 70 + 40 \\
500 \longrightarrow 400 + 100 \\
\end{array}
$$

$$14 + 110 + 500$$

 ©Curriculum Associates, LLC Copying is not permitted.

▶ **Connect It** **Make a ten and a hundred to add.**

7 Look at the first *Model It*. Write the value of the total hundreds, tens, and ones.

5 hundreds = _____   11 tens = _____   14 ones = _____

8 Look at the last *Model It*. How many ones, tens, and hundreds are there? Fill in the blanks.

14 = _____ ones   110 = _____ tens   500 = _____ hundreds

9 What is the same about the numbers in Problems 7 and 8? What is different?

_____

_____

10 What is the total number of rocks and minerals in the display? Show your work.

_____

▶ **Try It** **Try another problem.**

11 What is 649 + 184? Show your work.

_____

Practice ▸ **Adding Three-Digit Numbers**

Study the model below. Then solve Problems 12–14.

Example

There are 146 firefighters and 158 police officers marching in a parade. What is the total number of firefighters and police officers marching in the parade?

You can show your work on an open number line.

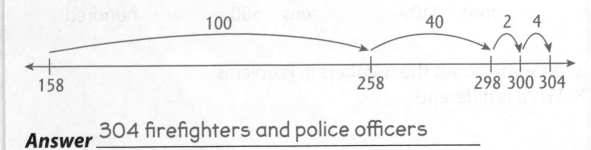

Answer <u>304 firefighters and police officers</u>

12 A basketball team sells 379 tickets before game day. Another 136 people buy tickets at the door. How many tickets does the team sell in all?

Show your work.

How many hundreds, tens, and ones does each number have?

Answer _____

©Curriculum Associates, LLC   Copying is not permitted.

13 Ms. Stone's students work in the school garden. They plant 267 beet plants and 278 onion plants. What is the total number of plants?

Show your work.

Remember, you can add in any order.

Answer _____

---

14 There is a box of foam shapes in the art room. It has 356 squares and 304 circles. Which addition problem shows how many foam shapes there are in all?

What does the 0 mean in 304?

A $600 + 5 + 10$

B $600 + 50 + 10$

C $600 + 90 + 6$

D $300 + 50 + 6$

Dean chose **A** as the answer. This answer is wrong. How did Dean get his answer?

_____

_____

_____

©Curriculum Associates, LLC   Copying is not permitted.

Practice **Adding Three-Digit Numbers**

Solve the problems.

1 How can you show 203 + 160?
Circle all the correct answers.

   A 300 + 60 + 3

   B 300 + 90

   C 200 + 100 + 60 + 3

   D 3 + 60 + 300

2 Jane writes 700 + 90 + 9 to add two three-digit
numbers. What two numbers could she be adding?
Circle the correct answer.

   A 354 + 455

   B 396 + 313

   C 521 + 278

   D 590 + 290

3 Find 563 + 127. Fill in the chart.
Then complete the equation.

Hundreds	Tens	Ones

_____ hundreds + _____ tens + _____ ones = _____

4 Write the missing numbers on the open number line. Then write the addition equation that the number line shows.

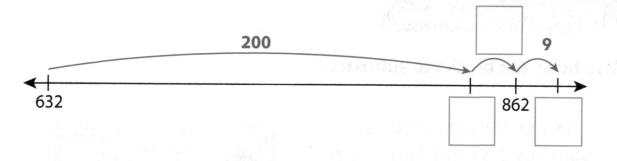

_____ + _____ = _____

Use the information in the box for Problems 5 and 6.

5 Carmen has 172 photos of her family. She also has 153 photos of friends. Which photo album will hold all of her pictures?

Show your work.

Choose an album!

Album A holds 225 photos.

Album B holds 275 photos.

Album C holds 375 photos.

6 Write your own problem about the photo albums in Problem 5. Have a partner solve your problem.

✓ **Self Check** **Now you can add three-digit numbers. Fill this in on the progress chart on page 59.**

Ⓖ Use What You Know

Use base-ten blocks to subtract.

Holly has 368 pet pal cards. Dora has 243 cards. How many more cards does Holly have than Dora?

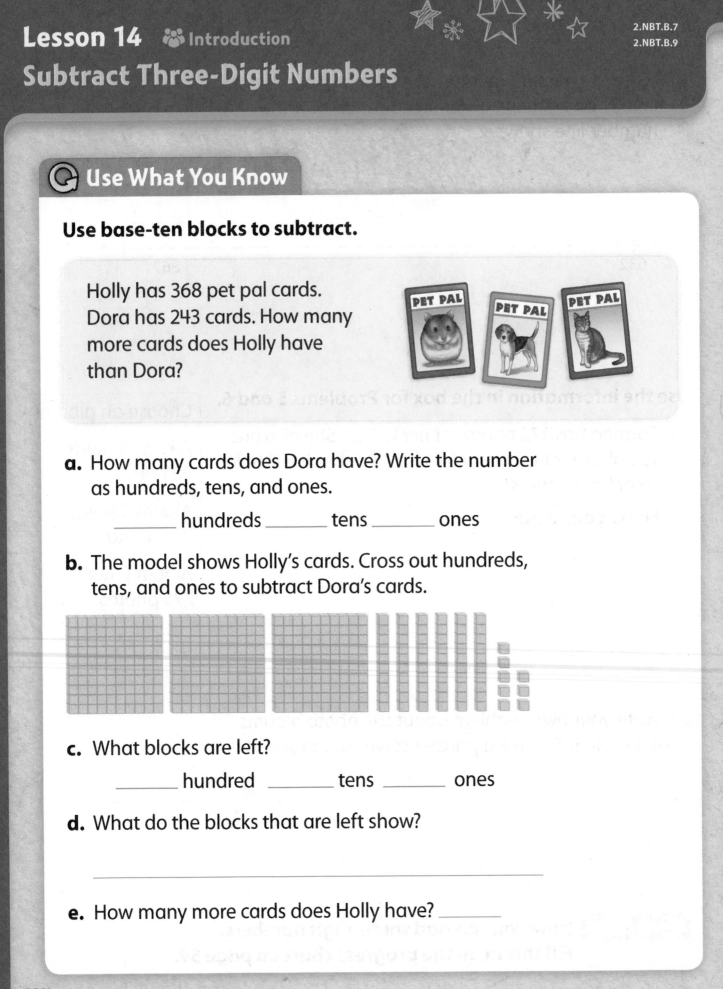

a. How many cards does Dora have? Write the number as hundreds, tens, and ones.

_____ hundreds _____ tens _____ ones

b. The model shows Holly's cards. Cross out hundreds, tens, and ones to subtract Dora's cards.

c. What blocks are left?

_____ hundred _____ tens _____ ones

d. What do the blocks that are left show?

_____

e. How many more cards does Holly have? _____

©Curriculum Associates, LLC   Copying is not permitted.

▷▷ Find Out More

Sometimes you have to regroup three-digit numbers to subtract.

There are enough hundreds, tens, and ones to subtract $368 - 243$ without regrouping.

100s	10s	1s
3	6	8
2	4	3

$3 > 2 \quad 6 > 4 \quad 8 > 3$

There are not enough ones in 368 to subtract 249 without regrouping.

100s	10s	1s
3	6	8
2	4	9

$3 > 2 \quad 6 > 4 \quad \boxed{8 < 9}$

You need more ones to subtract 9.

Regroup a ten in 368 to get 10 more ones.

100s	10s	1s
3	$\cancel{6}$ 5	18
− 2	4	9
1	1	9

Think:
$300 + 60 + 8 = 300 + 50 + 18$

The difference is 1 hundred, 1 ten, 9 ones, or 119.

▶ Reflect Work with a partner.

1 Talk About It Are there enough ones in 465 to subtract 328? What do you need to do?

Write About It _____

_____

_____

Learn About ▶ **Subtracting Hundreds, Tens, and Ones**

Read the problem. Then you will show subtraction in different ways.

There are 450 campers at Camp Cody. One day, 218 campers did art projects. The rest did sports. How many campers did sports that day?

▶ **Picture It** **You can subtract using base-ten blocks.**

Show 450.

Regroup 1 ten as 10 ones.

Then take away 218.

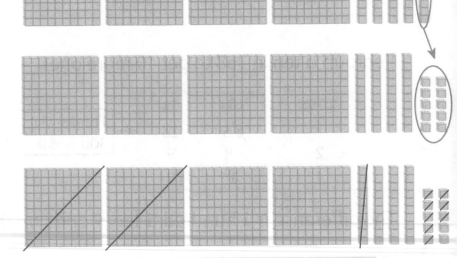

▶ **Model It** **You can subtract hundreds, tens, and ones.**

Think: 218 = **200 + 10 + 8**

$$\begin{array}{r} 450 \\ -\ 200 \\ \hline 250 \\ -\ 10 \\ \hline 240 \\ -\ 8 \\ \hline ? \end{array}$$

©Curriculum Associates, LLC   Copying is not permitted.

Connect It Find the difference.

2 Look at *Picture It*. Why do you need to trade
1 ten for 10 ones?

_____

_____

3 Fill in the boxes to find $450 - 218$.

$$400 \quad + \quad \boxed{} \quad + \quad 10$$
$$- \quad 200 \quad + \quad 10 \quad + \quad 8$$
$$\boxed{} \quad + \quad \boxed{} \quad + \quad \boxed{}$$

4 How many campers did sports? _____

5 **Talk About It** Look at *Model It*. How is the way the
problem is solved like the way shown in *Picture It*?
How is it different?

Write About It _____

_____

_____

_____

Try It Try another problem.

6 Jim has 572 stamps. Leo has 347 stamps. How
many more stamps does Jim have than Leo?
Show your work.

_____

_____

Learn About ▶ **Regrouping to Subtract**

Read the problem. Then you will model subtraction.

At Brown School, there are 305 girls and 276 boys.
How many more girls are there than boys?

▶ **Picture It** **You can use base-ten blocks to regroup.**

$305 = 300 + 5$

$305 = 200 + 100 + 5$

$305 = 200 + 90 + 15$

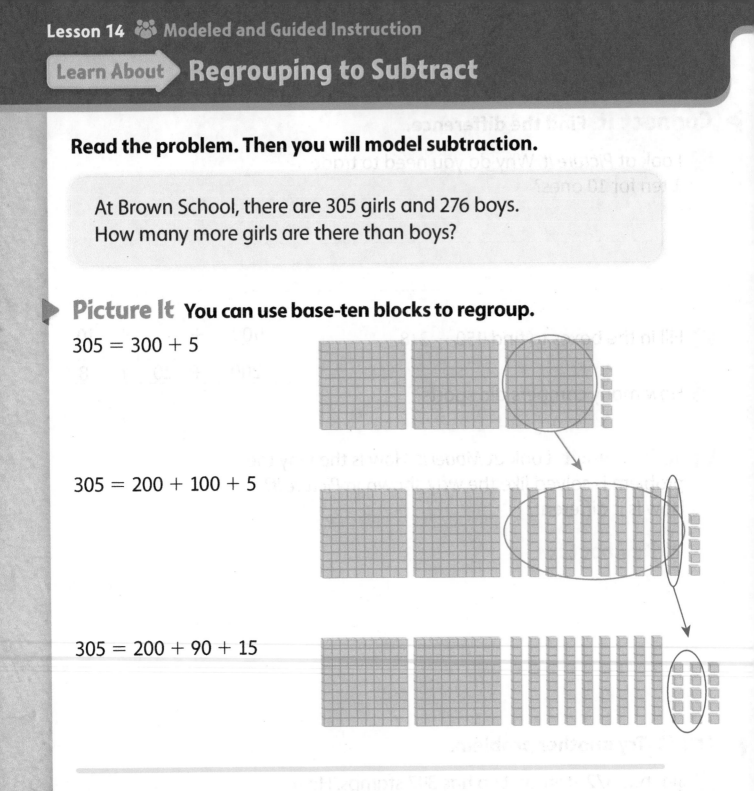

▶ **Model It** **You can use an open number line.**

Think of subtraction as addition: $276 + ? = 305$.

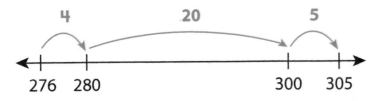

 ©Curriculum Associates, LLC   Copying is not permitted.

▶ **Connect It** **Subtract two different ways.**

7 Compare the digits in each place in 305 and 276.
Write < or > in each box.

3 hundreds + 0 tens + 5 ones
2 hundreds + 7 tens + 6 ones

3 [ ] 2   0 [ ] 7   5 [ ] 6

8 How can you tell from your answer to Problem 7
that you need to regroup two times?

_____

_____

9 How many hundreds, tens, and ones are
there after you regroup? Fill in the chart.
Then subtract.

10 How many more girls are there

than boys? _____

100s	10s	1s
[ ]	[ ]	[ ]
− 2	7	6
[ ]	[ ]	[ ]

▶ **Try It** **Try another problem.**

11 At Taylor School, students go to school for 180 days.
They have already been in school for 136 days. How
many school days are left? Show your work.

_____

_____

Practice ▶ **Subtracting Three-Digit Numbers**

Study the model below. Then solve Problems 12–14.

Example

Carla had 725 roses. She used some to make a float for a parade. Now she has 142 roses. How many roses did she use for the float?

You can show your work on a number line.

725 − 142 is the same as 142 + ? = 725

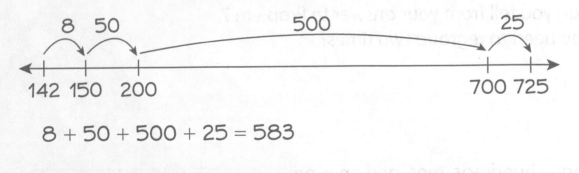

8 + 50 + 500 + 25 = 583

Answer ___Carla used 583 roses.___

12 Gus had 872 pennies. He gave 725 pennies to the pet shelter. How many pennies does Gus have left?

Show your work.

> Do you need to regroup? If so, how?

Answer _____

13 Students need to paint 500 pumpkins for the fair. They have painted 193 so far. How many pumpkins are left to paint?

Show your work.

How could you add up to find the answer?

Answer _____

---

14 Ms. Diaz had 185 stickers. She gave some away. Now she has 139 stickers. How many stickers did Ms. Diaz give away?

A 46

B 54

C 56

D 146

You can add or subtract to find the answer.

Ria chose **D** as the answer. This answer is wrong. How did Ria get her answer?

_____

_____

_____

©Curriculum Associates, LLC   Copying is not permitted.

Solve the problems.

1 For each subtraction problem, tell if you need to regroup tens to get more ones. Then tell if you need to regroup hundreds. Circle *Yes* or *No* for Tens and for Hundreds for each problem.

	Tens	Hundreds
a. 932 − 845	Yes No	Yes No
b. 673 − 581	Yes No	Yes No
c. 392 − 270	Yes No	Yes No
d. 557 − 148	Yes No	Yes No

2 Fill in the blanks to find 826 − 635.

100s	10s	1s
☐	12	6
− 6	3	5
☐	☐	☐

3 Kali had some shells. She found 132 more. Now she has 215 shells. How many shells did she have to begin with? Circle the correct answer.

A 83

B 123

C 223

D 347

©Curriculum Associates, LLC   Copying is not permitted.

4 Add up to find the difference. Fill in the blanks.

524 − 395 = ?

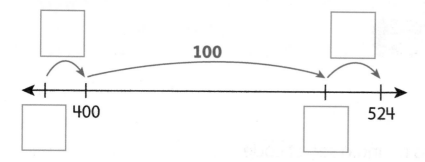

524 − 395 = _____

5 Any class that earns 750 reading points gets a pizza party. Which class has more points? How many more points?

Show your work.

Class	Reading Points
A	585
B	612

_____

6 Look at Problem 5. Ben says Class B needs 148 more points to get a pizza party. Is Ben correct? Explain.

_____

_____

_____

✓ **Self Check** **Now you can subtract three-digit numbers. Fill this in on the progress chart on page 59.**

Add Several Two-Digit Numbers

⟳ Use What You Know

Add three numbers.

Gia follows directions to find a secret code for a treasure hunt.

- Start at the oak tree. Take 36 steps toward the fence.

- Turn right. Take 28 steps.

- Turn left. Take 42 steps.

- The total number of steps is the secret code.

What is the secret code?

a. Break each number into tens and ones. Write your answers in the box.

$36 = \underline{\hspace{1cm}} + \underline{\hspace{1cm}}$

$28 = \underline{\hspace{1cm}} + \underline{\hspace{1cm}}$

b. Add the tens. What do you get? _____

$42 = \underline{\hspace{1cm}} + \underline{\hspace{1cm}}$

c. Add the ones. What do you get? _____

d. What is the secret code? Explain how you got your answer.

_____

_____

©Curriculum Associates, LLC   Copying is not permitted.

There are many ways to add three numbers.

You have learned how to break apart all three numbers and then add the tens and ones.

You can also add two numbers at a time.

$$36 \quad + \quad 28 \quad + \quad 42$$
$$64 \quad + \quad 42 \quad = 106$$

You can look for two numbers that make a ten.
Add those first. Then add the third number.

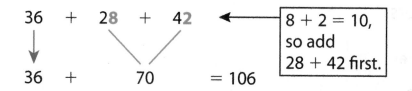

$$36 \quad + \quad 28 \quad + \quad 42$$

| 8 + 2 = 10, so add 28 + 42 first. |

$$36 \quad + \quad 70 \quad = 106$$

Sometimes there are two numbers that make 100.
Add these first. Then add the third number.

$$25 \quad + \quad 59 \quad + \quad 75$$
$$100 \quad + \quad 59 \quad = 159$$

▷ **Reflect** **Work with a partner.**

1 **Talk About It** Why would you change the order that you add three numbers? Explain using 37 + 21 + 63.

Write About It _____

_____

_____

Learn About Adding Four Two-Digit Numbers

Read the problem. Then you will explore different ways to add four numbers.

> Ray and Cho fill water balloons for a game. Ray fills 16 red balloons and 41 white balloons. Cho fills 22 red balloons and 39 white balloons. How many balloons do they fill in all?

▶ **Model It** **You can break the numbers into tens and ones.**

Break each number into tens and ones.
Then add pairs of numbers.

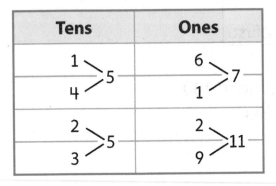

Tens	Ones
1 ⟩5 4	6 ⟩7 1
2 ⟩5 3	2 ⟩11 9

    5 + 5 tens   7 + 11 ones

▶ **Model It** **You can add two numbers at a time.**

Look for ones that make a 10.
Add those numbers first.

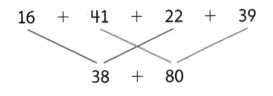

16 + 41 + 22 + 39

38 + 80

©Curriculum Associates, LLC   Copying is not permitted.

Connect It Add four two-digit numbers.

2 Look at the first *Model It*. Fill in the blanks to find the total number of balloons.

_____ tens + _____ ones = _____

3 The box shows how Ella added the numbers. How is this like adding in the first *Model It*?

$$\begin{array}{r} 10 + 6 \\ 40 + 1 \\ 20 + 2 \\ 30 + 9 \\ \hline 100 + 18 \end{array}$$

_____

_____

_____

4 Look at the second *Model It*. Why are 41 and 39 grouped together?

_____

_____

5 Complete the work in the second *Model It* to find the number of balloons Ray and Cho fill in all.

_____

Try It Try another problem.

6 Yuri's bowling scores are 45, 62, 68, and 55. What is the total of Yuri's four scores? Show your work.

_____

Practice ▶ **Adding Several Two-Digit Numbers**

Study the model below. Then solve Problems 7–9.

Example

Mr. Carey's class took a nature walk. The chart shows what they collected. How many objects did they collect in all?

Rocks	Pinecones	Feathers	Acorns
52	37	12	63

You can add two numbers at a time.

$37 + 63 = 100$

$52 + 12 = \underline{64}$

164

Answer _The class collected 164 objects._

---

7 There are 28 parrots and 23 macaws in the zoo's jungle birdhouse. There are also 22 toucans and 25 hornbills. What is the total number of birds?

Show your work.

Do any ones digits make a ten?

Answer _____

©Curriculum Associates, LLC   Copying is not permitted.

8 It is race day at the city park. The chart shows how many people sign up for each race. What is the total number of people who sign up?

1-Mile Race	Bike Race	Swim Race
66	49	37

You can break the numbers into tens and ones.

Show your work.

Answer _____

---

9 Gita adds the number of cans in the school recycling bins. What is the total?

$28 + 16 + 32 + 2 = ?$

A 68

B 76

C 78

D 96

How many tens are in each number?

Jeff chose **D** as the answer. This answer is wrong. How did Jeff get his answer?

_____

_____

_____

Practice ▸ **Adding Several Two-Digit Numbers**

Solve the problems.

1 Complete each equation using a number from the box at the right.

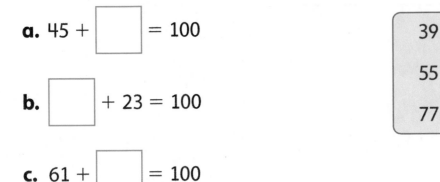

a. $45 + \boxed{} = 100$

b. $\boxed{} + 23 = 100$

c. $61 + \boxed{} = 100$

| 39 |
| 55 |
| 77 |

2 A train has four cars. The number of people in each car is 25, 18, 24, and 15. Which of the sentences below are true? Circle all the correct answers.

A The number of people in two of the cars add up to 40.

B More than 100 people are on the train.

C Fewer than 100 people are on the train.

D There are 82 people on the train.

3 A park has 25 oak trees, 25 maple trees, 25 elm trees, and 32 pine trees. What is the total number of trees? Circle the correct answer.

A 57

B 97

C 107

D 117

©Curriculum Associates, LLC   Copying is not permitted.

Use these number cards for Problems 4–6.

| 27 | 48 | 43 | 29 | 34 | 35 |

4 Pablo picks two cards with ones digits that make a ten. Which two cards does he pick? Explain.

_____

_____

5 Pablo loses the 29 card. Taj picks three of the cards that are left. His cards have a sum less than 100. What are the three cards? Show how to find the sum by adding tens and ones.

_____

_____

6 Explain how you decided which cards to use for Problem 5. Check your answer by adding two numbers at a time.

_____

_____

 **Self Check** **Now you can add many two-digit numbers. Fill this in on the progress chart on page 59.**

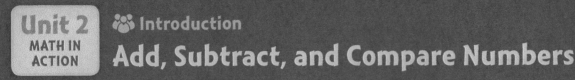

Study an Example Problem and Solution

**Read this problem about adding numbers.
Then look at Sweet T's solution to the problem.**

Cookie Order

Sweet T is in the Bake Stars' kitchen.
He takes notes about a cookie order.

Cookie Order

- Make between 400 and 500 cookies.
- Make chocolate chip, peanut butter, and oatmeal cookies.
- Make the same number of each kind of cookie.

How many of each kind of cookie should the Bake Stars make? Show why your numbers work.

Show how Sweet T's solution matches the checklist.

Problem-Solving Checklist

☐ Tell what is known.

☐ Tell what the problem is asking.

☐ Show all your work.

☐ Show that the solution works.

a. Circle something that is known.

b. Underline something that you need to find.

c. Draw a box around what you do to solve the problem.

d. Put a checkmark next to the part that shows the solution works.

©Curriculum Associates, LLC Copying is not permitted.

Sweet T's Solution

Hi, I'm Sweet T. Here's how I solved this problem.

▷ **I know** there are 3 kinds of cookies.
The total is between 400 and 500 cookies.

▷ **I need to find** 3 numbers that have a sum between 400 and 500.

Try 100: 100 + 100 + 100 = 300.
Try 200: 200 + 200 + 200 = 600.

Using 100 makes too few cookies. Using 200 makes too many cookies.

▷ 150 is between 100 and 200.

▷ **I can make a quick drawing** to help me add.

I drew 100 + 100 + 100 and 50 + 50 + 50.

▷ 300 + 100 + 50 = 450 and 450 is between 400 and 500.

The numbers total 450. So 150 works.

▷ **Here is what the Bake Stars can make:**

150 chocolate chip cookies
150 peanut butter cookies
150 oatmeal cookies

Try **Another Approach**

There are many ways to solve problems. Think about how you might solve the Cookie Order problem in a different way.

Cookie Order

Sweet T is in the Bake Stars' kitchen.
He takes notes about a cookie order.

Cookie Order
- Make between 400 and 500 cookies.
- Make chocolate chip, peanut butter, and oatmeal cookies.
- Make the same number of each kind of cookie.

How many of each kind of cookie should the Bake Stars make? Show why your numbers work.

▶ **Plan It** **Answer this question to help you start thinking about a plan.**

Look at the numbers for each kind of cookie in the sample answer. Could you use numbers greater than these? Less than these? Explain.

_____

_____

_____

_____

©Curriculum Associates, LLC   Copying is not permitted.

Solve It Find a different solution for the Cookie Order problem. Show all your work on a separate sheet of paper.

You may want to use the problem-solving tips to get started.

Problem-Solving Tips

- **Models**

Hundreds	Tens	Ones
1	?	?

Problem-Solving Checklist

Make sure that you . . .

☐ tell what you know.

☐ tell what you need to do.

☐ show all your work.

☐ show that the solution works.

- **Word Bank**

add	subtract	total	greater than
sum	difference	compare	less than

- **Sentence Starters**

  • I can look for numbers _____

  • I can try numbers _____

Reflect

Use Mathematical Practices Talk about this question with a partner.

- **Reason with Numbers** How can the numbers in the sample answer help you solve this problem?

Discuss ▸ **Models and Strategies**

**Solve the problem on a separate sheet of paper.
There are different ways you can solve it.**

Cookie Boxes

Sweet T is packing an order of 145 chocolate chip
cookies. The pictures below show the different-size
boxes there are at the shop. Each box holds a
different number of cookies.

How can Sweet T pack the cookies?

©Curriculum Associates, LLC   Copying is not permitted.

▶ Plan It and Solve It   Find a solution to Sweet T's Cookie Boxes problem.

Decide which boxes Sweet T should use to pack the cookies.
- Tell why you chose these boxes.
- Show that your answer works.

You may want to use the problem-solving tips to get started.

Problem-Solving Tips

- **Questions**
  - Would I rather use fewer boxes or more boxes?
  - Do I want to make sure that every box I use is full?

- **Word Bank**

add	sum	total
hundred	tens	ones

- **Sentence Starters**
  - I can use _____ boxes.
  - The box holds _____
  - I used these boxes because _____

Problem-Solving Checklist

Make sure that you . . .
- ☐ tell what you know.
- ☐ tell what you need to do.
- ☐ show all your work.
- ☐ show that the solution works.

▶ Reflect

Use Mathematical Practices Talk about this question with a partner.

- **Make an Argument** How can you explain the reason for the boxes that you chose?

Solve the problem on a separate sheet of paper.

Fruits and Vegetables

Sweet T likes to talk about numbers with the Bake Stars.

Here are some of the things he said at the end of last month.

- We used more than 200 pounds of vegetables this month.
- We used less than 300 pounds of fruit this month.
- The total amount of fruit and vegetables we used was between 500 and 550 pounds.

How many pounds of fruit could the Bake Stars have used? How many pounds of vegetables?

▶ **Solve It** **Find the amount of fruit and vegetables that the Bake Stars could have used.**

- Tell how many pounds of fruit they might have used.
- Tell how many pounds of vegetables they might have used.
- Show that the total weight is between 500 and 550 pounds.

▶ **Reflect**

Use Mathematical Practices Talk about this question with a partner.

- **Be Precise** How did you use words or symbols to show that your answer works?

©Curriculum Associates, LLC   Copying is not permitted.

Fruit Salads

Sweet T found a mistake that the Bake Stars made. They made 448 fruit salads for a customer. The customer only ordered 248 fruit salads. Here is what they plan to do with the extra food.

- Donate some fruit salads to the youth center.
- Keep some fruit salads at the shop. Give them out for free to customers.

How many fruit salads should the Bake Stars donate? How many should they give out for free?

▶ ## Solve It Decide what to do with the extra fruit salads.

- Tell how many to give to the youth center.
- Tell how many to keep at the shop.
- Explain why your numbers work.

▶ ## Reflect

Use Mathematical Practices Talk about this question with a partner.

- **Make Sense of Problems** What was the first thing that you did to solve this problem? Why?

Solve the problems.

1 Compare each number below to 436.

    442   430   398   535

Write each number in the correct box below.

Less Than 436	Greater Than 436

2 Shelby has 517 baseball cards and 386 football cards.
She wants to find how many cards she has in all.
How could she add 517 + 386?
Circle all the correct answers.

A 386 + 51 + 7

B 500 + 300 + 10 + 80 + 7 + 6

C 517 + 300 + 80 + 6

D 800 + 90 + 13

3 Paige solved a subtraction problem. She had to regroup
tens to subtract ones. She did not regroup hundreds.
Which of these could be the problem Paige solved?
Circle all the correct answers.

A	**B**	**C**	**D**
236	520	634	862
− 118	− 427	− 251	− 523

©Curriculum Associates, LLC   Copying is not permitted.

4 Mrs. Foster has 30 apples. She uses 12 apples to make apple pies. How many apples does she have left?

Show your work by adding up.

Answer _____ apples

5 Ken's book has 343 pages. He has read 228 pages. How many pages does Ken have left to read?

Draw a model and write an equation to solve the problem.

Answer _____ pages

6 Complete the table to show 863 in different ways. In the last row, show a way that is different from the others.

Hundreds	Tens	Ones
8		3
0		3
6	6	

Performance Task

Answer the questions. Show all your work on separate paper.

Four students want to order tickets to play their favorite games at the school fair. They have to order some packs of 100, some sheets of 10, and some single tickets.

- The table below shows the total number of tickets each student wants.

- Copy the table onto a separate sheet of paper.

How many packs of 100, sheets of 10, and single tickets can the students order to get the total number of tickets they want? Fill in your table.

Checklist

Did You . . .

☐ use place value correctly?

☐ check your answers?

☐ explain your answers with words and numbers?

Name	Packs of 100	Sheets of 10	Single Tickets	Total
Lori				555
Penn				662
Maria				656
Antoine				593

Reflect

Look for Structure How did you use what you know about place value to solve this problem?

©Curriculum Associates, LLC   Copying is not permitted.

Unit 3
Measurement and Data

Real-World Connection You use measurements in many parts of your life. You and a friend might measure your heights. You subtract to find how much taller you are. Maybe you have 30 minutes for lunch each day. You might have 8 coins that are worth 48 cents.

In This Unit You will learn how to use measurement tools. You will measure lengths using different units. You will also compare measurements like length, time, and money.

Let's learn about different measurement tools and units.

✓ Self Check

Before starting this unit, check off the skills you know below.

I can:	Before this unit	After this unit
use a ruler to measure an object.	☐	☐
choose the correct tool for measuring an object.	☐	☐
measure the same object using different units.	☐	☐
estimate the length of an object.	☐	☐
compare lengths to tell which object is longer and how much longer it is.	☐	☐
add and subtract lengths to solve problems.	☐	☐
measure lengths and show data on a line plot.	☐	☐
draw and solve problems with pictographs and bar graphs.	☐	☐
tell and write time to the nearest 5 minutes.	☐	☐
solve problems about money.	☐	☐

©Curriculum Associates, LLC   Copying is not permitted.

Lesson 16 👥 Introduction

Understand Length and Measurement Tools

💭 Think It Through

What does it mean to measure length?

You can find the length of objects, like a marker.

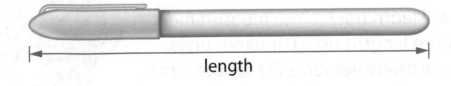

length

Think You can use objects to measure length.

You can use paper clips to measure the length of a marker.

Line up the edge of the first paper clip with the edge of the marker.

- Do not put the marker in the middle of the paper clips. ✗
- Do not use paper clips that are different sizes. ✗
- Do not have any spaces between the paper clips. ✗
- Do not have any paper clip on top of another paper clip. ✗

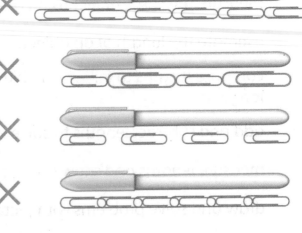

✏️ How many paper clips fit under the marker? _____

©Curriculum Associates, LLC Copying is not permitted.

Think You can use units of the same size to measure objects.

Inches and centimeters are two units used to measure length.

The length of a quarter is about 1 **inch** (in.).

Your little finger is about 1 **centimeter** (cm) across.

1 inch is a little longer than 2 centimeters.

A ruler is a tool used to measure length.

inches												
0	1	2	3	4	5	6	7	8	9	10	11	12

centimeters
0 1 2 3 4 5 6 7 8 9 10 11 12 13 14 15 16 17 18 19 20 21 22 23 24 25 26 27 28 29 30

This ruler is not life-sized.

 Reflect **Work with a partner.**

1 **Talk About It** Why would you measure the length of your shoe with a ruler instead of paper clips?

Write About It _____

_____

_____

_____

Think About ▷ **Measuring with Tiles and Rulers**

🔍 **Let's Explore the Idea** **You can use 1-inch tiles to help you understand a ruler.**

2 Use the tiles your teacher gives you to find the length of the yarn.

How many tiles did you use? _____

3 Each tile is 1 inch long.

How long is the yarn? _____

4 Number the tiles you used in order from 1 to 6.

5 Place Tile 1 above the ruler below. Place it so the left side of the tile lines up with 0.
Then put the other tiles in order next to Tile 1.

6 What do you notice about the numbers on your tiles and on the ruler?

_____

©Curriculum Associates, LLC   Copying is not permitted.

Let's Talk About It
Work with a partner.

7 Where do you put the first tile when you measure the yarn?

_____

8 How do you find the length of the yarn using tiles?

_____

_____

9 Use your ruler to measure the yarn. What number on the ruler should you line up with the left end of the yarn? _____

10 Now how do you find the length of the yarn?

_____

_____

Try It Another Way **Now use 1-centimeter tiles.**

11 Use 1-centimeter tiles to measure the length of this yarn. How many tiles do you use? _____

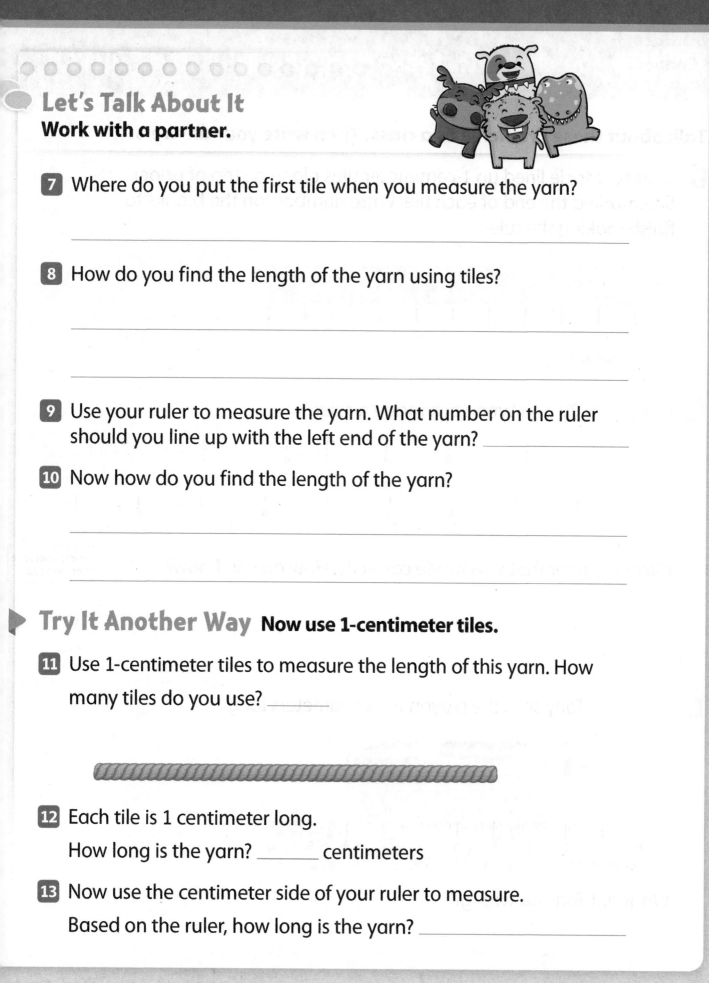

12 Each tile is 1 centimeter long.

How long is the yarn? _____ centimeters

13 Now use the centimeter side of your ruler to measure.

Based on the ruler, how long is the yarn? _____

Connect ▶ **Ideas About Measuring with Tiles and Rulers**

Talk about these problems as a class. Then write your answers.

14 **Create** Macie lined up 1-centimeter tiles along a strip of paper. She marked the end of each tile. Write numbers on the blanks to finish making the ruler.

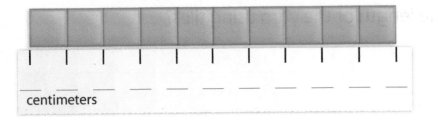

centimeters

15 **Compare** Ty and Lynn each made a ruler.

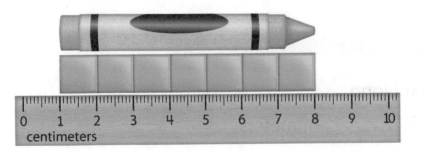

Circle the ruler that was made correctly. How do you know?

These rulers are not life-sized.

_____

16 **Analyze** Tony says the crayon is 8 centimeters long.

What did Tony do wrong?

_____

©Curriculum Associates, LLC Copying is not permitted.

Apply ▶ **Ideas About Measuring with Tiles and Rulers** 159

Put It Together **Use what you have learned to complete this task.**

17 For this task, you will need 1-inch tiles and 1-centimeter tiles.

Part A Use 1-inch tiles to make a ruler.

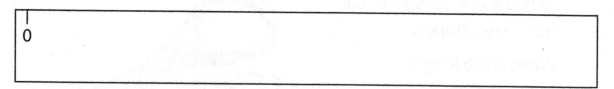

How long is your ruler? _____

Part B Use 1-centimeter tiles to make a ruler.

How long is your ruler? _____

Part C Explain the steps you took to make the rulers.

_____

_____

_____

_____

↻ Use What You Know

Review how a ruler measures length.

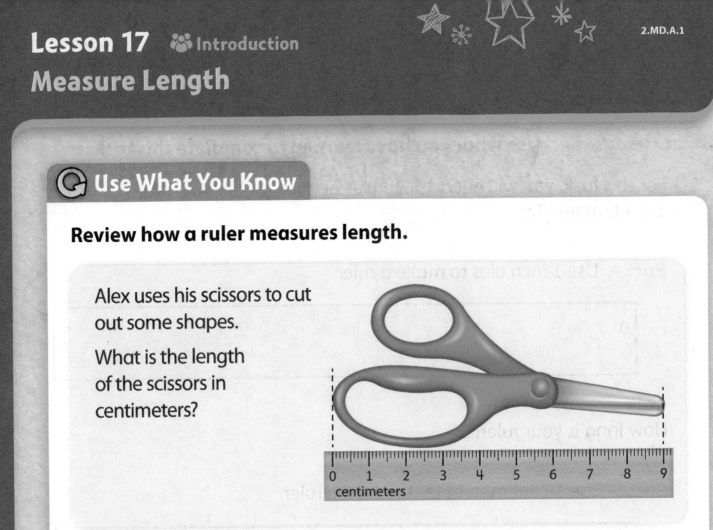

Alex uses his scissors to cut out some shapes.

What is the length of the scissors in centimeters?

centimeters

a. What units are shown on the ruler? _____

b. What number is lined up with the handle of the scissors? _____

c. How do you use a ruler to measure the scissors?

_____

_____

_____

d. What is the length of the scissors?

_____

©Curriculum Associates, LLC   Copying is not permitted.

Rulers often show both inches and centimeters.

Many rulers show 12 inches. This is equal to 1 **foot**.

This ruler is not life-sized.

How many inches are on the ruler? _____

How many centimeters are on the ruler? _____

Some measuring tools are longer than a ruler.

- A yardstick shows 36 inches.
  There are 36 inches in a **yard**.

- A meter stick shows 100 centimeters.
  There are 100 centimeters in a **meter**.

- A tape measure can show inches
  and centimeters.

▶ **Reflect** **Work with a partner.**

1 Talk About It How is a yardstick like an inch ruler?
How is it different?

Write About It _____

_____

_____

Learn About ▶ **Measuring Length**

Read the problem. Then you will look at ways to measure.

> Erin wants to measure the length of a sheet of notebook paper. What is the length in inches?

▶ **Measure It** **You can use 1-inch tiles to find the length.**

Line up the edge of the paper with the first tile.

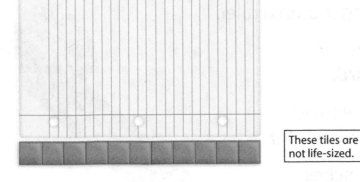

These tiles are not life-sized.

▶ **Measure It** **You can use a ruler to find the length.**

Line up the edge of the paper with the 0 on the inch ruler.

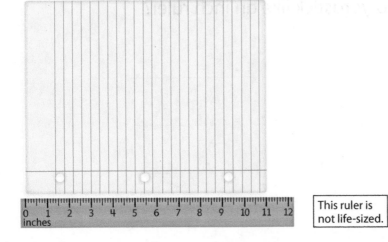

This ruler is not life-sized.

©Curriculum Associates, LLC   Copying is not permitted.

▶ **Connect It** **Use the models to solve the problem.**

2 Look at the first *Measure It*. How many inch tiles
are used? _____

3 Look at the second *Measure It*. What is the length
of the paper? _____

4 Do you think it is easier to measure with tiles
or a ruler? Explain.

_____

_____

5 **Talk About It** Would the length of the paper
be the same if you measured it using a yardstick?
Why or why not?

Write About It _____

_____

_____

▶ **Try It** **Measure the key using centimeters.**

6 Look at the centimeter tiles. The key has
a length of _____ centimeters.

7 Look at the centimeter ruler. The key has
a length of _____ centimeters.

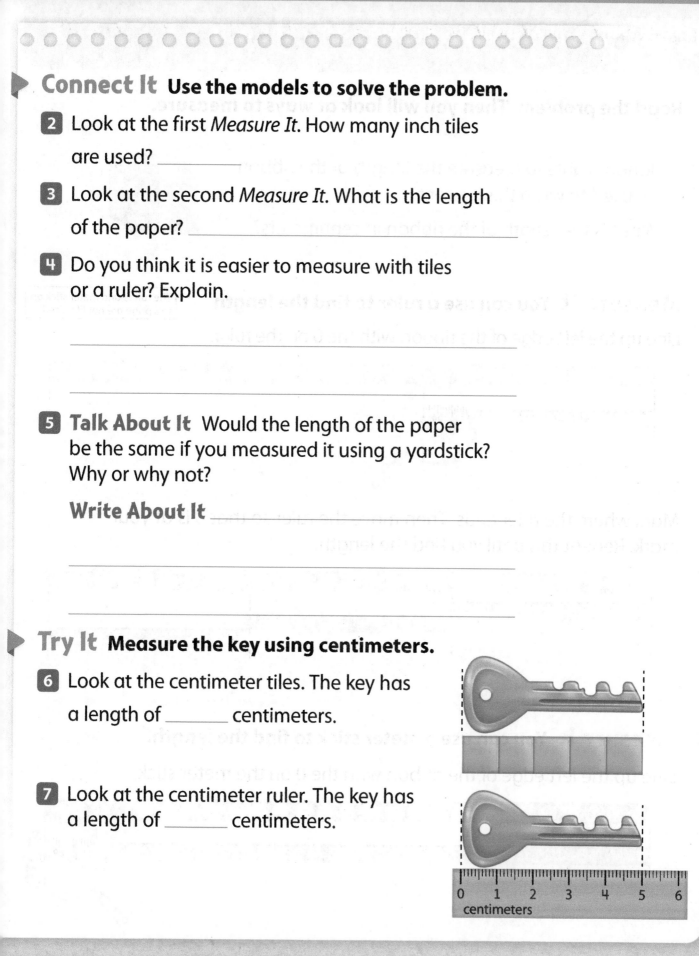

©Curriculum Associates, LLC   Copying is not permitted.

Learn About ▷ More Ways to Measure Length

Read the problem. Then you will look at ways to measure.

Jonah wants to measure the length of the ribbon he used to wrap this present.

What is the length of the ribbon in centimeters?

▶ **Measure It** **You can use a ruler to find the length.**

> The rulers and meter stick on this page are not life-sized.

Line up the left edge of the ribbon with the 0 on the ruler.

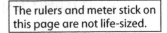

Mark where the ruler ends. Then move the ruler so that 0 is at your mark. Repeat this until you find the length.

▶ **Measure It** **You can use a meter stick to find the length.**

Line up the left edge of the ribbon with the 0 on the meter stick.

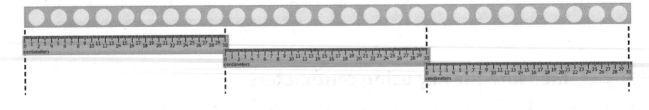

©Curriculum Associates, LLC Copying is not permitted.

▶ **Connect It** **Use the models to solve the problem.**

8 Look at the first *Measure It*. The length of the ribbon is equal to how many rulers? _____

9 How many centimeters are on each ruler? _____

10 Write an equation to find the length of the ribbon.

_____ cm + _____ cm + _____ cm = _____ cm

11 Look at the meter stick. How long is the ribbon?

_____ centimeters

12 **Talk About It** Why is it easier to measure the ribbon with a meter stick than with a ruler?

Write About It _____

_____

_____

_____

▶ **Try It** **Try another problem.**

13 Circle the objects that are easier to measure with a centimeter ruler. Underline the objects that are easier to measure with a meter stick.

a hot dog   a jump rope   a pencil

              your height   this book

Practice ▸ Measuring Length

Study the model below. Then solve Problems 14–16.

Example

Dawson found a shell. How long is the shell in centimeters?

You can use a centimeter ruler. Make sure to line up the shell at 0.

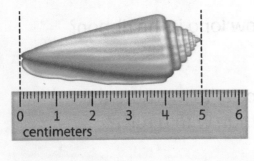

Answer _____5_____ centimeters

---

14 Measure the length of the eraser in inches using a ruler.

ERASER

Answer _____ inches

What side of the ruler should you use?

©Curriculum Associates, LLC   Copying is not permitted.

15 Think about the length of the actual objects. Draw lines to match each object with the best tool for measuring it.

a watch

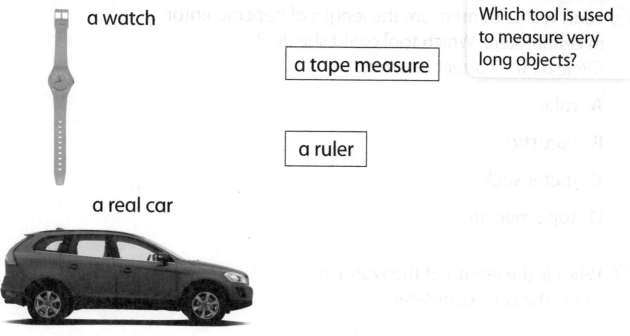

a tape measure

a ruler

Which tool is used to measure very long objects?

a real car

---

16 What is the length of the craft stick in inches?

A 4 inches

B 5 inches

C 10 inches

D 11 inches

Jake chose **C** as the answer. This answer is wrong. How did Jake get his answer?

_____

_____

Did Jake measure with a unit that is smaller or bigger than inches?

Practice **Measuring Length**

Solve the problems.

1 Leah wants to measure the length of her calculator in centimeters. Which tool could she use? Circle all the correct answers.

A ruler

B yardstick

C meter stick

D tape measure

2 What is the length of the worm in inches? Circle the correct answer.

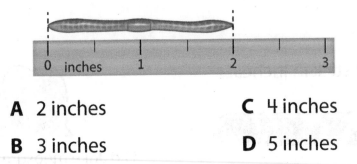

A 2 inches

C 4 inches

B 3 inches

D 5 inches

3 Ruby measured each line in centimeters. She wrote the length of each line next to it. Did she measure correctly? Choose *Yes* or *No* for each length.

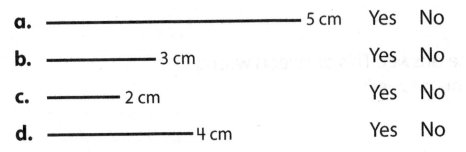

a. ———————— 5 cm   Yes   No

b. ————— 3 cm   Yes   No

c. ——— 2 cm   Yes   No

d. ————— 4 cm   Yes   No

©Curriculum Associates, LLC   Copying is not permitted.

4 Marcus says the length of the stick is 6 centimeters.
What did Marcus do wrong?
Circle the correct answer.

A He measured in inches.

B He used the wrong side of the ruler.

C He didn't line up one end of the stick at 0.

D He should have used a yardstick.

5 Kayla started to draw a rectangle that is 4 inches
long. Complete Kayla's rectangle to make it the
correct length.

6 Brian wants to measure the length of his bed in
centimeters. He says the best tool to use is a ruler.
Do you agree? Why or why not?

_____

_____

_____

✓ **Self Check** **Now you can solve problems using a ruler.
Fill this in on the progress chart on page 153.**

💭 Think It Through

What happens when you measure the same object in both inches and feet?

Kim measures a piece of fabric. She says that the length is 24 inches.

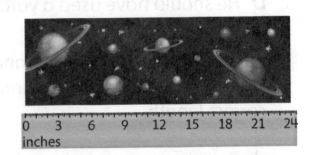

Nadia measures the same piece of fabric. She says that the length is 2 feet.

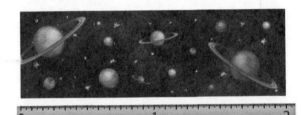

Think It takes different numbers of each unit to measure an object.

Kim's number and Nadia's number are different.

🖊 Did the length of the fabric change? _____

The girls measured using different units.

Kim measured in inches.
The fabric has a length of 24 inches.

Nadia measured in feet.
The fabric has a length of 2 feet.

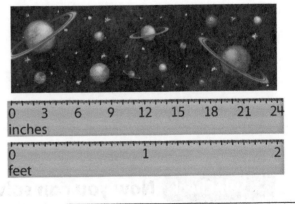

The yardsticks on this page are not life-sized.

©Curriculum Associates, LLC   Copying is not permitted.

Think It takes more of a smaller unit to measure an object.

Think about the fabric on the previous page.
It took 24 inches to measure the fabric.
But it only took 2 feet to measure the fabric.

Look at the ruler. Which unit is greater,
1 inch or 1 foot?

When you measure in feet, you say "1 foot" instead of "1 feet." Say "feet" if the length is not 1.

_____

A ruler showing inches 0 through 12.

12 inches = 1 foot

This ruler is not life-sized.

An inch is shorter than a foot.

So you need more inches than feet to measure the fabric.

▶ Reflect Work with a partner.

1 **Talk About It** Josie measured the length of her bed using both centimeters and meters. Did it take more meters or more centimeters to measure its length?

Write About It _____

_____

_____

Think About ▶ **Comparing Units of Measure**

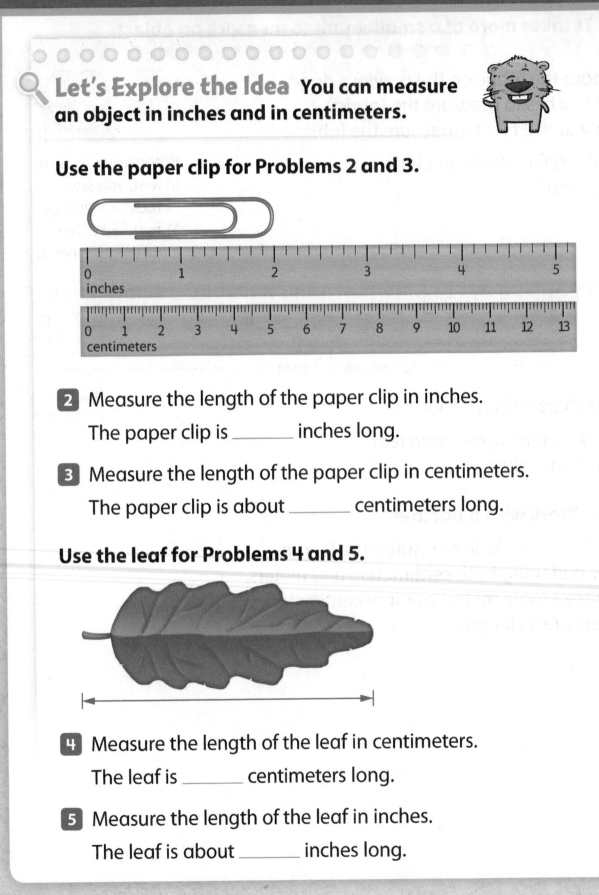

🔍 **Let's Explore the Idea** You can measure an object in inches and in centimeters.

Use the paper clip for Problems 2 and 3.

2 Measure the length of the paper clip in inches.

The paper clip is _____ inches long.

3 Measure the length of the paper clip in centimeters.

The paper clip is about _____ centimeters long.

Use the leaf for Problems 4 and 5.

4 Measure the length of the leaf in centimeters.

The leaf is _____ centimeters long.

5 Measure the length of the leaf in inches.

The leaf is about _____ inches long.

©Curriculum Associates, LLC Copying is not permitted.

Let's Talk About It

Work with a partner.

6 Does it take fewer inches or fewer centimeters to measure the length of the paper clip?

_____

7 Does it take fewer inches or fewer centimeters to measure the length of the leaf?

_____

8 If you measure the length of your math book, will it take fewer inches or fewer centimeters? Why?

_____

_____

▶ Try It Another Way **Compare other units.**

9 Would it take fewer erasers or fewer buttons to measure the length of your pencil?
Circle the correct answer.

10 Would it take more hair clips or more crayons to measure the length of your desk?
Circle the correct answer.

Talk about these questions as a class. Then write your answers.

11 Analyze Ed measures a picture using combs and quarters as his units. The length of the picture is 3 units of one item and 18 units of the other. Which item does he use to get a length of 3 units? Explain.

_____

_____

12 Compare Joe's bedroom is 4 yards long. He also measures it in feet. Is the length of Joe's bedroom more yards or more feet? Explain.

_____

_____

_____

13 Explain Kit's red ribbon is 12 inches long. Her blue ribbon is 12 centimeters long. Kit says they are the same length. Do you agree? Explain.

_____

_____

_____

Apply ▶ **Ideas About Comparing Units of Measure**

Put It Together **Use what you have learned to complete this task.**

14 Eric measures the length of his model car.

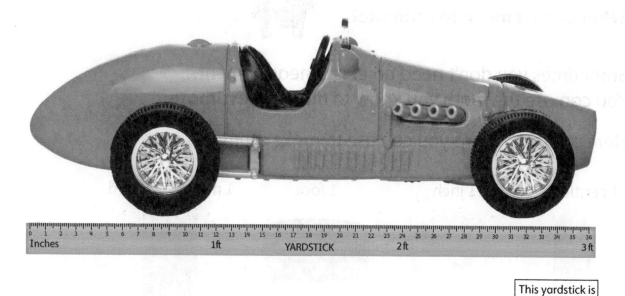

This yardstick is not life-sized.

Part A What is the length of Eric's car? _____ feet

Part B What is the length of Eric's car? _____ yard(s)

Part C Which units would you need the most of to measure the length of Eric's car?
Circle the correct answer.

     inches   centimeters   yards   feet

Part D Which units would you need the least of to measure the length of Eric's car?
Circle the correct answer.

     inches   centimeters   yards   feet

Lesson 19 👥 Introduction
Understand Estimating Length

Think It Through

What does it mean to estimate?

Sometimes you don't need an exact measurement.
You can use the math you know to make an **estimate**.

Here are some items you can use to make estimates.

1 centimeter	1 inch	1 foot	1 meter or 1 yard

about the width of your little finger | about the width of a quarter | about the length of a loaf of bread | about the width of a door

Think Use what you know about units to estimate length.

Ty wants to estimate the length of his toy car.
He thinks about 2 quarters would fit under his car.

✏️ Is the length of the toy car longer or shorter

than 2 quarters? _____

✏️ What do you think is a good estimate for the length

of Ty's car in inches? _____

©Curriculum Associates, LLC Copying is not permitted.

Think Use measurements you already know to estimate length.

Julia wants to estimate the length of her pencil box.
She knows a marker is about 14 centimeters long.

Julia thinks about how a marker would look next
to her pencil box.

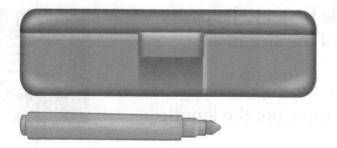

Which best describes the length of the pencil box?
Mark all the correct answers.

☐ less than 14 cm   ☐ more than 14 cm

☐ less than 28 cm   ☐ more than 28 cm

▶ Reflect Work with a partner.

1 Talk About It Hannah estimates that Julia's pencil box is
30 centimeters long. Is this a good estimate? Explain why or why not.

Write About It _____

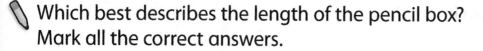

_____

_____

Think About ▷ **Using Different Units to Estimate Length**

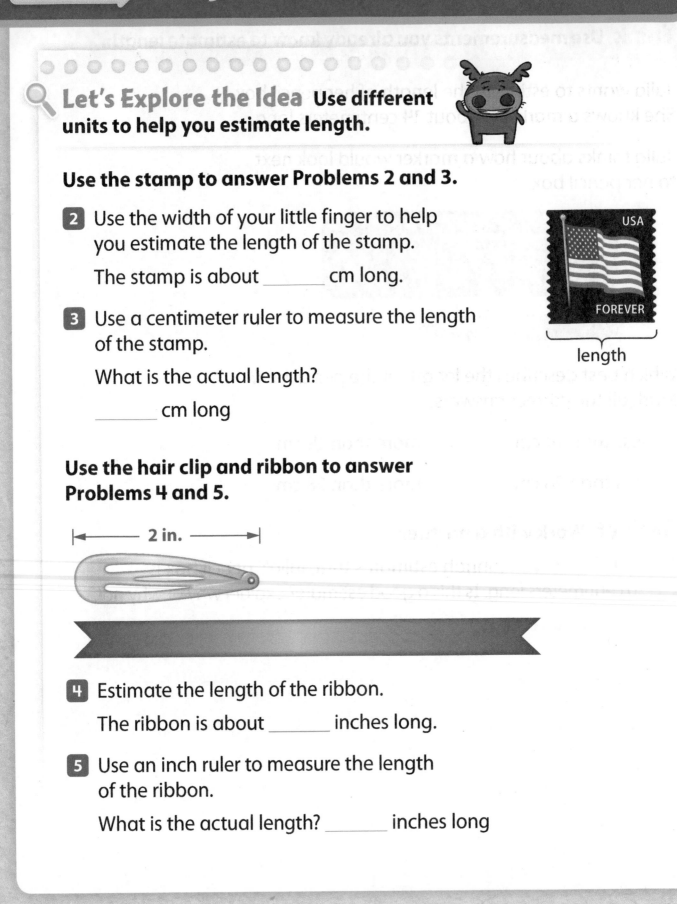

🔍 **Let's Explore the Idea** Use different units to help you estimate length.

Use the stamp to answer Problems 2 and 3.

2 Use the width of your little finger to help you estimate the length of the stamp.

The stamp is about _____ cm long.

3 Use a centimeter ruler to measure the length of the stamp.

What is the actual length?

_____ cm long

length

Use the hair clip and ribbon to answer Problems 4 and 5.

|← 2 in. →|

4 Estimate the length of the ribbon.

The ribbon is about _____ inches long.

5 Use an inch ruler to measure the length of the ribbon.

What is the actual length? _____ inches long

©Curriculum Associates, LLC Copying is not permitted.

Let's Talk About It
Solve the problems below as a group.

6 How did you estimate the length of the stamp?

_____

7 How did you estimate the length of the ribbon?

_____

_____

8 How does your estimate compare with the actual length of the ribbon?

_____

_____

9 **Talk About It** **Work with a partner.**
When would you estimate a length instead of measuring the exact length?

Write About It _____

_____

▶ Try It Another Way Estimate length using different units.

10 The length of your teacher's desk

Estimate: _____ feet   Actual: _____ feet

11 The length of a classroom wall

Estimate: _____ meters   Actual: _____ meters

Connect ▶ **Ideas About Estimating Length**

Talk about these questions as a class. Then write your answers.

12 Explain Estimate the length of your arm. Use one of the units in the box to make your estimate.

Write your estimate. Explain how you made your estimate.

centimeters
inches
feet
meters

_____

_____

_____

13 Analyze Erik estimates that the length of a crayon is about 4 inches. He measures the crayon and says it has a length of 10 inches. Do you think his estimate or his measurement is wrong? Why?

_____

_____

_____

14 Identify Which is the best estimate for the length of a see-saw? Mark your answer.

☐ 30 inches   ☐ 100 yards   ☐ 4 meters

Explain how you made your estimate.

_____

_____

_____

©Curriculum Associates, LLC   Copying is not permitted.

Apply ▶ **Ideas About Estimating Length**

Put It Together **Use what you have learned to complete the task.**

15 Mrs. Chen made the list of lengths at the right.

Part A Estimate the length of an object in your classroom. Use an item from Mrs. Chen's list to help you estimate. Record your choices below.

Lengths of Items	
new pencil	19 centimeters
sticky note	3 inches
egg carton	1 foot
door height	2 meters

My object: _____

Item used for estimate: _____

My estimate: _____

Part B Explain how you found your estimate.

_____

_____

_____

Part C Use a ruler, a yardstick, or a meter stick to measure the actual length of your object.

Actual length of object: _____

Part D How does the actual length compare with your estimate?

_____

_____

_____

🔄 Use What You Know

You know how to measure length.

Layla found this spoon and fork with her tea set.

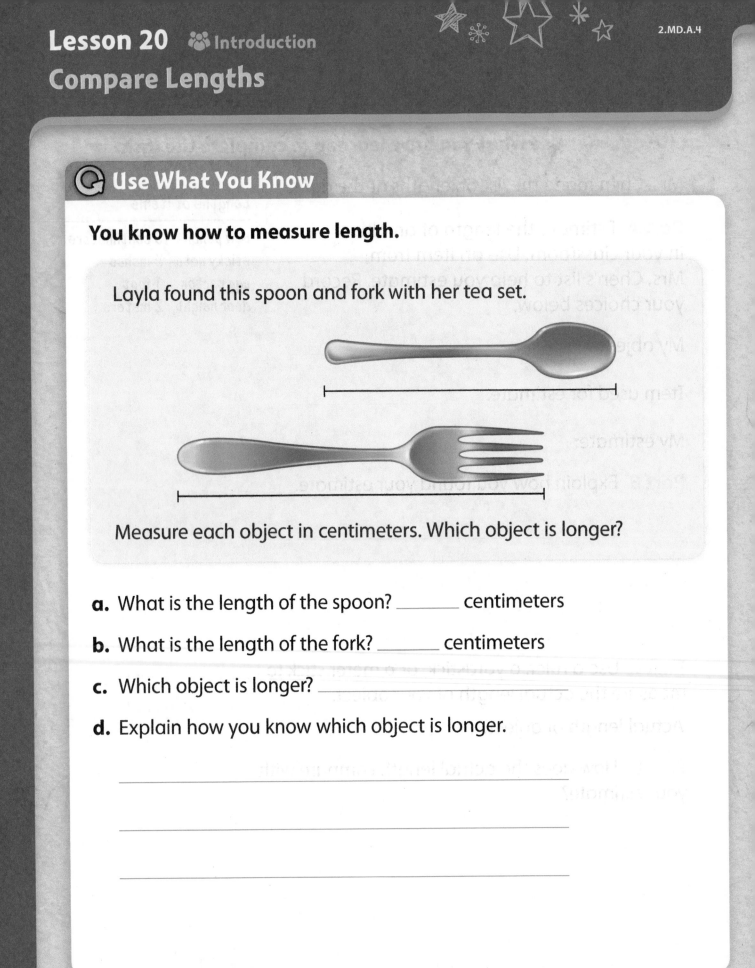

Measure each object in centimeters. Which object is longer?

a. What is the length of the spoon? _____ centimeters

b. What is the length of the fork? _____ centimeters

c. Which object is longer? _____

d. Explain how you know which object is longer.

_____

_____

_____

©Curriculum Associates, LLC   Copying is not permitted.

What is the difference between the length of the spoon and the length of the fork?

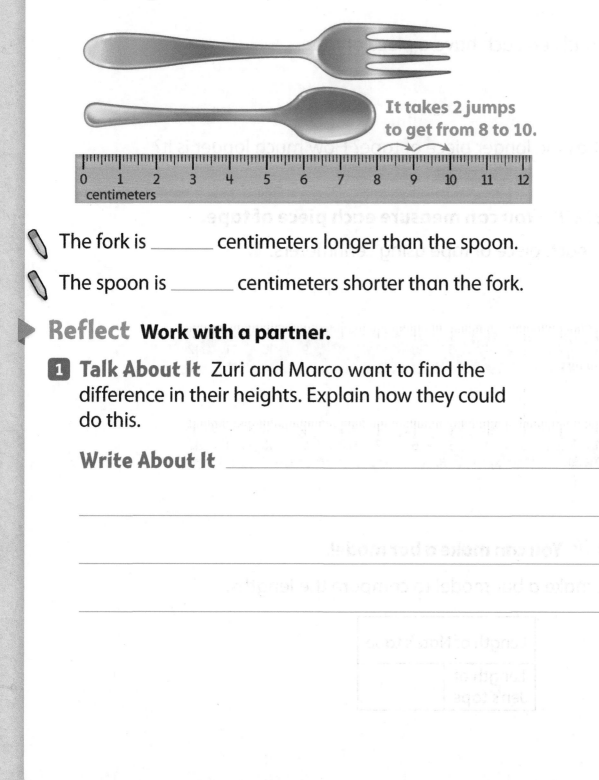

It takes 2 jumps to get from 8 to 10.

The fork is _____ centimeters longer than the spoon.

The spoon is _____ centimeters shorter than the fork.

▶ **Reflect** **Work with a partner.**

1 **Talk About It** Zuri and Marco want to find the difference in their heights. Explain how they could do this.

Write About It _____

_____

_____

_____

Learn About ▶ **Finding Differences Between Lengths**

Read the problem. Then you will explore ways to find the difference between lengths.

Nate and Jen each have a piece of tape.

Nate   Jen

Who has the longer piece of tape? How much longer is it?

▶ **Measure It** **You can measure each piece of tape.**

Measure each piece of tape using centimeters.

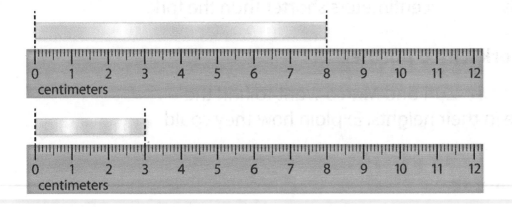

▶ **Model It** **You can make a bar model.**

You can make a bar model to compare the lengths.

Length of Nate's tape	
Length of Jen's tape	?

©Curriculum Associates, LLC   Copying is not permitted.

▶ **Connect It** **Write an equation to find the difference.**

2 What is the length of each person's piece of tape?
Write the numbers in the bar model.

Length of Nate's tape	
_____ centimeters	
Length of Jen's tape	?
_____ centimeters	

3 Who has the longer piece of tape? Explain how
you know.

_____

4 Write an equation you can use to find the difference
in the lengths. Then find the difference.

_____

5 Complete the sentence to compare Nate's and Jen's tape.

_____ tape is _____ centimeters

longer than _____ tape.

▶ **Try It** **Try another problem.**
Use these stickers for Problems 6 and 7.

6 Circle the sticker that is longer.

7 Measure and write the length
of each sticker in centimeters.
How much longer is the long
sticker than the short sticker?

_____

_____

Learn About ▶ **Ways to Compare Lengths**

Read the problem. Then you will explore ways to compare lengths.

How much shorter in inches is the eraser than the crayon?

▶ **Measure It** **You can measure each object and find the difference.**

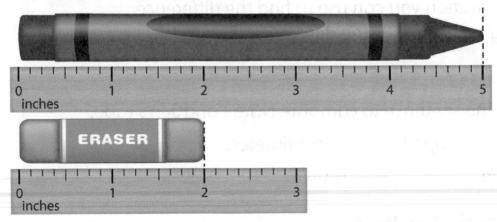

▶ **Measure It** **You can measure the difference.**

Line up one end of the eraser and the crayon.
Then use a ruler to measure the difference.

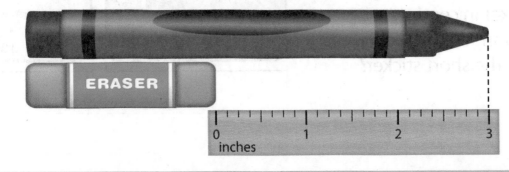

©Curriculum Associates, LLC Copying is not permitted.

Connect It Find the difference.

8 Look at the first *Measure It*. Explain how to find how much shorter the eraser is than the crayon.

_____

_____

9 How much shorter is the eraser than the crayon?

_____

10 What is measured in the second *Measure It*?

_____

_____

11 Talk About It Kelly says that you cannot always use the method shown in the second *Measure It*. Do you agree? Why or why not?

Write About It _____

_____

_____

Try It Try another problem.

12 Henry has two paper clips.

Circle the paper clip that is shorter. How many inches shorter is it?

_____

Practice ▷ **Comparing Lengths**

Study the model below. Then solve Problems 13–15.

Example

Jonah is 52 inches tall. His sister Sophia is 43 inches tall. How much taller is Jonah than Sophia?

You can show your work with a bar model and equation.

$$52 - 43 = 9$$

52	
43	?

Answer _Jonah is 9 inches taller than Sophia._

---

13 Anna measures the paper strips below in centimeters. What is the difference in the lengths of the paper strips?

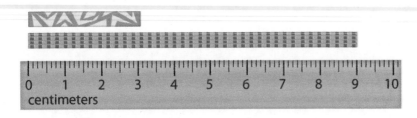

> The difference in the lengths of the paper strips is how much longer or shorter one is than the other.

Show your work.

Answer _____

©Curriculum Associates, LLC Copying is not permitted.

14 Circle the nail that is shorter. Then tell how much shorter it is. Measure using centimeters.

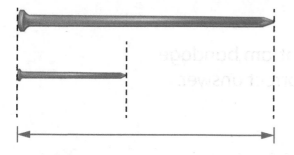

What equation can you write to help you find the answer?

Show your work.

Answer _____

---

15 Tim has a piece of yarn that is 3 inches long. Which piece of yarn is 1 inch shorter than Tim's yarn?

A ▰▰▰▰▰▰▰▰▰▰▰▰▰▰▰▰▰

B ▰▰▰▰

C ▰▰▰▰▰▰▰▰▰▰

D ▰▰▰▰▰▰▰▰

Will the length of the correct piece of yarn be more or less than 3 inches?

Ben chose **A** as the answer. This answer is wrong. How did Ben get his answer?

_____

_____

_____

Practice ▶ **Comparing Lengths**

Solve the problems.

1 How much longer in inches is the bottom bandage than the top bandage? Circle the correct answer.

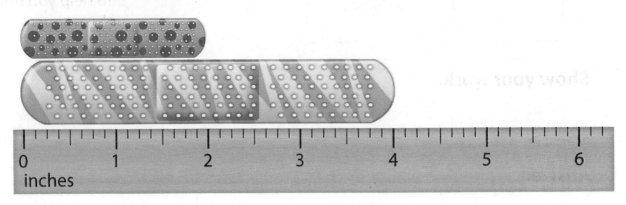

A 2 inches

B 3 inches

C 4 inches

D 5 inches

2 The tail on Evan's kite is 85 centimeters long. The tail on Maya's kite is 68 centimeters long. What equation could you use to find the difference in the lengths? Circle all the correct answers.

A $85 + 68 = ?$

B $85 - 68 = ?$

C $85 + ? = 68$

D $68 + ? = 85$

 ©Curriculum Associates, LLC Copying is not permitted.

3 What is the difference in the lengths of the two straws? Measure using centimeters. Circle the correct answer.

A 3 cm   **C** 7 cm

B 4 cm   **D** 11 cm

4 A table is 10 feet long. A desk is 3 feet long. Circle *True* or *False* for each statement.

a. The table is 7 feet shorter than the desk.   True   False

b. The table is 7 feet longer than the desk.   True   False

c. The desk is 7 feet shorter than the table.   True   False

d. The desk is 7 feet longer than the table.   True   False

5 Draw a line that is 6 centimeters longer than the line below.

How long is your line in centimeters? How did you know the length your line should be?

✓ **Self Check** **Now you can compare lengths.**
Fill this in on the progress chart on page 153.

Ⓖ Use What You Know

You know how to compare lengths.

The length of a toy alligator's body is 32 inches.
The tail of the alligator is 6 inches shorter than the body.
How long is the tail?

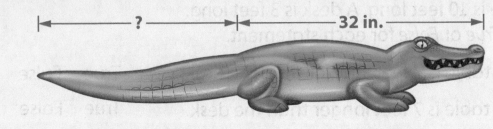

a. What is the length of the alligator's body?

_____

b. Will you add or subtract to find the length of the
alligator's tail? Why?

_____

_____

c. Write an equation to find the length of the tail.

_____

d. How long is the alligator's tail? _____

©Curriculum Associates, LLC   Copying is not permitted.

You can add lengths to find a total length.

You can measure the tail and measure the body.
Then add to find the total length of the alligator.

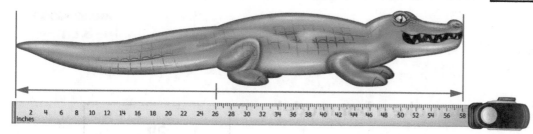

> When you add lengths, the units need to be the same.

26 inches   +   32 inches

You can also measure the whole alligator.

> The tape measures on this page are not life-sized.

You get the same answer either way.

 26 inches + 32 inches = _____ inches

▷ Reflect Work with a partner.

1 Talk About It Why does adding the lengths of the parts of the alligator give you the same answer as measuring the whole alligator?

Write About It _____

_____

©Curriculum Associates, LLC   Copying is not permitted.

Learn About ▸ Solving Problems About Lengths

Read the problem. Then you will explore ways to model it.

> Michaela has a string of beads that is 56 centimeters long. She cuts off 8 centimeters to make it the right length for a necklace. How long is the string of beads now?

▸ **Picture It You can draw a picture.**

The string of beads is **56** centimeters long.

Michaela cuts off **8** centimeters.

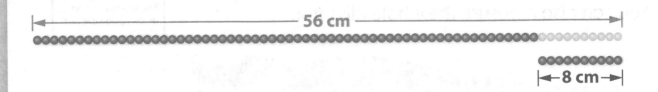

▸ **Model It You can make a bar model.**

The total length is **56** centimeters.

The part cut off is **8** centimeters.

56	
?	8

▸ **Model It You can use a number line.**

Start at **56**. Subtract to get a ten.
Then subtract the rest.

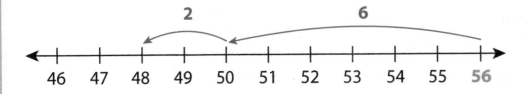

  ©Curriculum Associates, LLC Copying is not permitted.

Connect It Add and subtract lengths.

2 Look at the models on the previous page. Write a subtraction equation you can use to solve the problem.

_____

3 Write an addition equation you can use to solve the problem.

_____

4 Explain how the jumps on the number line show that Michaela cuts off 8 centimeters.

_____

_____

5 How long is the string of beads now? _____

6 How much shorter is a string of beads that is 34 centimeters long than a string that is 56 centimeters long? Explain how you found your answer.

_____

_____

Try It Try another problem.

7 Jesse threw a ball 59 feet. Owen threw a ball 15 feet less than Jesse. How far did Owen throw the ball?

_____

Learn About Solving Two-Step Problems About Length

Read the problem. Then you will explore ways to model it.

Sam and Sadie are making a poster with a border. Sam has a piece of border 23 inches long. Sadie has a border that is 7 inches longer than Sam's. The top of their poster is 50 inches long. Do they have enough border to cover the top of the poster? Explain your reasoning.

▶ **Picture It You can draw a picture.**

Sam's border   Sadie's border

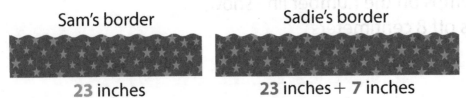

23 inches   23 inches + 7 inches

▶ **Model It You can use an open number line.**

Start at **23**. Add **7** first to get to the next ten.

To add 23 more, jump **20** and then **3**.

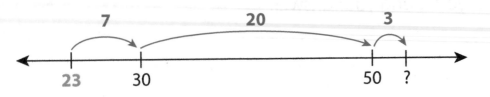

▶ **Model It You can use a diagram.**

Add **23 + 7** first to make a ten.

| 23 | 23 | 7 |

$$23 + 23 + 7$$
$$23 + \quad 30$$

©Curriculum Associates, LLC   Copying is not permitted.

► **Connect It** **Add and subtract lengths.**

8 Explain how you know the length of Sadie's border is 23 + 7.

_____

_____

9 Write an equation you can use to find the length of the two pieces together.

_____

10 Do Sam and Sadie have enough border to cover the top of the poster? Explain why or why not.

_____

_____

11 Ethan has two pieces of border. One is 24 inches long, and the other is 5 feet long. He says that the total length is 29 inches. What did he do wrong?

_____

► **Try It** **Try another problem.**

12 Sarah bought 18 yards of rope. She used 6 yards to hang a swing and 4 yards to hang a birdfeeder. How much rope is left? Show your work.

_____

Practice ▶ **Adding and Subtracting Lengths**

Study the model below. Then solve Problems 13–15.

Example

Mr. Yee walks 12 feet from his house to the sidewalk. Then he walks 28 feet to the mailbox. Mr. Yee turns around and walks 17 feet back toward his house along the sidewalk. How far does Mr. Yee have to walk to get back to his house now?

Look at how you can show your work with a bar model.

12	28
17	?

$$\begin{array}{r} 12 \\ + 28 \\ \hline 30 \\ + 10 \\ \hline 40 \end{array} \qquad \begin{array}{r} 40 \\ - 17 \\ \hline 30 \\ - 7 \\ \hline 23 \end{array}$$

Answer Mr. Yee has to walk 23 feet to get to his house.

---

13 Jude's sunflower grew 8 inches this week. It is 26 inches tall now. How tall was Jude's sunflower at the beginning of the week?

Show your work.

Was the sunflower taller or shorter at the beginning of the week?

Answer _____

©Curriculum Associates, LLC   Copying is not permitted.

14 A path in the park was 22 meters long. Then another section was added. Now the path is 50 meters long. How long is the new section?

Show your work.

Does the path get longer or shorter?

Answer _____

---

15 Lisa used 37 centimeters of string to hang a picture and 46 centimeters of string to hang another picture. She has 12 centimeters of string left. How much string did she start with?

The amount of string at the start is the amount of string Lisa used plus what other amount?

A 21 cm

B 71 cm

C 83 cm

D 95 cm

Chase chose **C** as the answer. This answer is wrong. How did Chase get his answer?

_____

_____

_____

©Curriculum Associates, LLC   Copying is not permitted.

Practice ▸ **Adding and Subtracting Lengths**

Solve the problems.

1 Maddie's dresser is 44 inches shorter than her bedroom wall. The length of the dresser is 36 inches. What is the length of the wall?
Circle the correct answer.

A 8 inches

B 12 inches

C 70 inches

D 80 inches

2 Jordan has two tracks for his toy cars. One track is 25 inches longer than the other. What could be the lengths of the tracks? Circle all the correct answers.

A 12 inches and 13 inches

B 75 inches and 50 inches

C 20 inches and 45 inches

D 5 inches and 20 inches

3 Willa draws three lines.

- a blue line that is 55 cm long

- a red line 14 cm shorter than the blue line

- a green line 23 cm shorter than the red line

What is the length of the green line?
Circle the correct answer.

A 18 cm

B 22 cm

C 32 cm

D 41 cm

 ©Curriculum Associates, LLC   Copying is not permitted.

4 Bella hangs a string of lights in her room. Then she adds two more strings of lights that are 12 feet and 9 feet long. Altogether, the length of all the lights is 32 feet. How long is the first string of lights?

Fill in the blanks. Then circle all the answers that show a step in solving the problem.

A $12 + 9 =$ _____   **C** $21 + 32 =$ _____

B $12 - 9 =$ _____   **D** $32 - 21 =$ _____

5 Josh was on a path 100 meters long. He ran 35 meters and then started walking. He ran again for the last 15 meters. How far did Josh walk?

Show your work.

Answer _____

6 Write a word problem that uses lengths. Then solve your problem.

_____

_____

✓ **Self Check** **Now you can add and subtract lengths. Fill this in on the progress chart on page 153.**

Understand Reading and Making Line Plots

Think It Through

What is a line plot?

A **line plot** is a way to organize a set of measurements, like the lengths of young sea lions at an aquarium.

52 inches   49 inches   50 inches   52 inches   52 inches   48 inches   49 inches

Think You can use a number line to make a line plot.

A number line is like a ruler or tape measure.

- The numbers have equal spaces between them.
- The numbers are in order.
- No numbers are skipped.

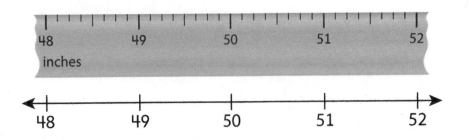

Circle the lengths of the shortest and longest sea lions on the ruler and the number line.

©Curriculum Associates, LLC   Copying is not permitted.

Think A line plot can help you show measurements.

This line plot shows the lengths of sea lions.

The number line starts at 48 because the shortest length is 48 inches.

✏️ Why does the number line end at 52? _____

_____

There are 7 lengths, so there should be 7 *X*s on the line plot.

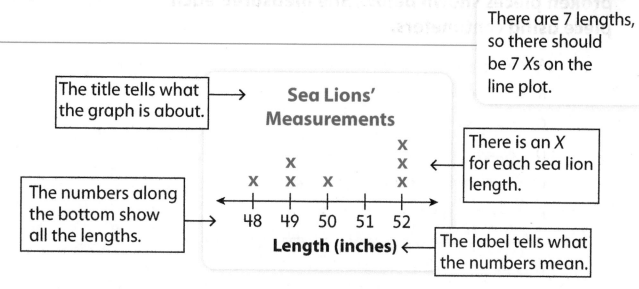

The title tells what the graph is about.

Sea Lions' Measurements

There is an *X* for each sea lion length.

```
                              X
                 X            X
        X   X    X            X
     ←——+———+———+———+———+———→
        48  49  50  51  52
```

The numbers along the bottom show all the lengths.

Length (inches)

The label tells what the numbers mean.

The line plot shows that 2 sea lions are 49 inches long.

▶ Reflect Work with a partner.

1 Talk About It How is the number line on a line plot like a ruler? How is it different?

Write About It _____

_____

_____

_____

Think About ▶ **Reading and Making Line Plots**

🔍 **Let's Explore the Idea** Measure lengths and make a line plot.

Julia spilled a box of spaghetti. She picked up the broken pieces shown below. She measured each piece using centimeters.

A ▬▬▬▬▬▬▬▬▬

B ▬▬▬▬▬

C ▬▬▬▬▬▬▬▬▬▬

D ▬▬▬▬▬▬

E ▬▬▬▬▬▬▬▬

F ▬▬▬▬▬▬▬▬▬

G ▬▬▬▬▬▬▬▬▬▬

H ▬▬▬▬▬▬▬▬

2 What is the length of piece A? _____ centimeters

3 Draw an X above that number on the line plot below.

4 Measure the rest of the spaghetti pieces. After you measure each piece, draw an X above the correct number on the line plot below.

Spaghetti Pieces

```
◄──┼────┼────┼────┼────┼────┼────►
   4    5    6    7    8    9    10
            Length (cm)
```

   ©Curriculum Associates, LLC   Copying is not permitted.

Let's Talk About It
Work with a partner.

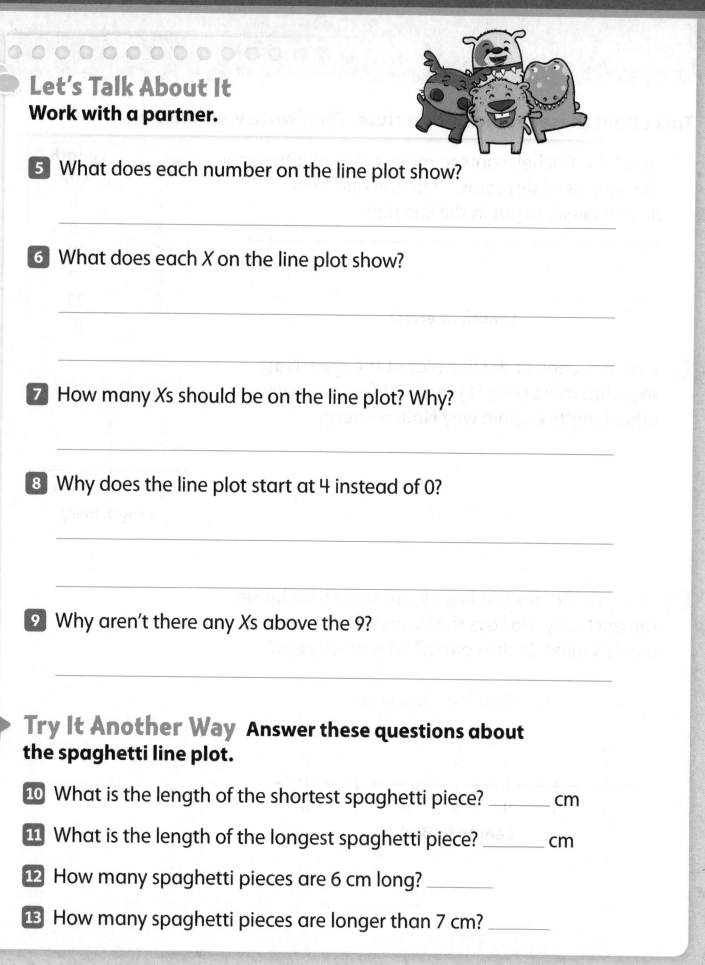

5 What does each number on the line plot show?

_____

6 What does each X on the line plot show?

_____

_____

7 How many Xs should be on the line plot? Why?

_____

8 Why does the line plot start at 4 instead of 0?

_____

_____

9 Why aren't there any Xs above the 9?

_____

▶ **Try It Another Way** **Answer these questions about the spaghetti line plot.**

10 What is the length of the shortest spaghetti piece? _____ cm

11 What is the length of the longest spaghetti piece? _____ cm

12 How many spaghetti pieces are 6 cm long? _____

13 How many spaghetti pieces are longer than 7 cm? _____

Connect ▸ **Ideas About Line Plots**

Talk about these problems as a class. Then write your answers.

14 Identify Rachel wants to make a line plot to show the lengths of six rooms. Write the numbers Rachel needs to put in the line plot.

Room	Length (meters)
A	8
B	6
C	10
D	9
E	11
F	10

☐ ☐ ☐ ☐ ☐ ☐

Length (meters)

15 Explain Look at the line plot at the right. Nate says that more people jumped 4 feet than any other length. Explain why Nate is wrong.

Long Jump Results

```
             X
   x         X
   x         X        X
   x         X        X
   |─────────|────────|
   3         4        5
```

Length (feet)

_____

_____

_____

16 Analyze Bo made a line plot to show how far he ran each day. Tia says the farthest Bo ran in one day is 3 miles. Is she correct? Why or why not?

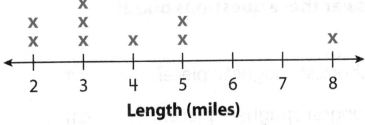

Bo's Running Distances

_____

_____

Apply Ideas About Line Plots

Put It Together Use what you have learned to complete this task.

17 Use the page of shells your teacher gives you.

Part A Measure the length of each shell in inches. Write the lengths in the table.

Part B Use your measurements to make a line plot.

Shell	Length (inches)
A	
B	
C	
D	
E	
F	
G	

Length (_____)

Part C The length of the longest shell is _____ inches.
The length of the shortest shell is _____ inches.

The length with the most shells is _____ inches.

Part D Two more shells are each 4 inches long. Explain how the line plot would change if the lengths of these shells were added to the line plot.

_____

_____

_____

⟳ Use What You Know

You know how to add and subtract to solve problems.

Parker asked his friends to tell him their favorite vegetable.
He organized their answers in a **pictograph**.

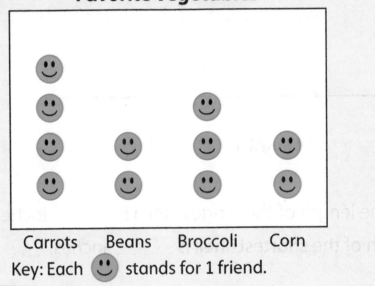

Favorite Vegetables

Carrots   Beans   Broccoli   Corn

Key: Each 🙂 stands for 1 friend.

a. How many faces are above the word "Carrots"? _____

> This tells how many friends chose carrots.

b. How many faces are above the word "Beans"? _____

> This tells how many friends chose beans.

c. Write an equation to find how many
friends chose carrots and beans in all.

_____ + _____ = _____

d. Write an equation to find how many more
friends chose carrots than beans.

_____ − _____ = _____

©Curriculum Associates, LLC   Copying is not permitted.

A **bar graph** uses bars to show information.

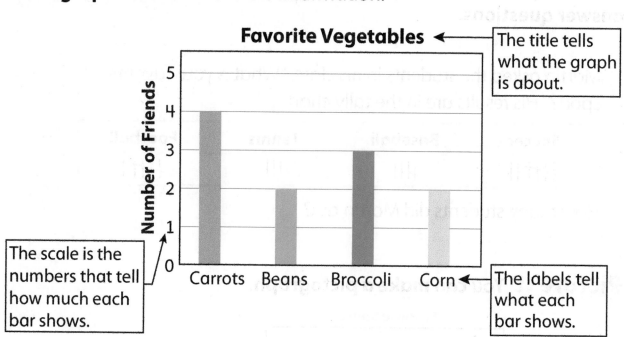

Favorite Vegetables ← The title tells what the graph is about.

Number of Friends

5
4
3
2
1
0

Carrots   Beans   Broccoli   Corn ← The labels tell what each bar shows.

The scale is the numbers that tell how much each bar shows.

The information shown in graphs is called **data**.

Reflect Work with a partner.

1 Talk About It How are the Favorite Vegetables pictograph and bar graph alike? How are they different?

Write About It _____

_____

_____

_____

©Curriculum Associates, LLC   Copying is not permitted.

Learn About ▷ **Using a Pictograph and Bar Graph**

Read the problem. Then you will use the graphs to answer questions.

Martin asked the students in his class, "What is your favorite sport?" His results are in the tally chart.

Soccer	Baseball	Tennis	Football
⦀⦀⦀ II	IIII	III	⦀⦀⦀ I

How many students did Martin ask?

▷ **Picture It** **You can make a pictograph.**

Favorite Sports

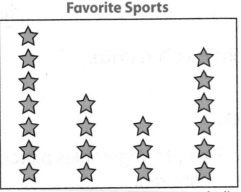

Soccer Baseball Tennis Football

Key: Each ⭐ stands for 1 student.

▷ **Model It** **You can make a bar graph.**

Favorite Sports

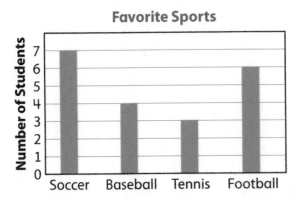

©Curriculum Associates, LLC   Copying is not permitted.

▶ **Connect It** **Use the graphs.**

2 How do you use the pictograph to find the
number of students who chose soccer?

_____

3 How do you use the bar graph to find the number
of students who chose soccer?

_____

_____

4 How many students chose soccer as their favorite? _____

5 Explain how to use the bar graph to find the total
number of students Martin asked.

_____

_____

6 How many students did Martin ask? Show your work.

_____

_____

▶ **Try It** **Try more problems.**

7 How many fewer students chose tennis than football? _____

8 Two students changed their answers from soccer to baseball.

Now how many students chose soccer? _____

Now how many students chose baseball? _____

Learn About ▷ **Making Bar Graphs and Pictographs**

Read the problem. Then you will show the data in a graph.

Lynn visited an apple orchard. She looked at one row of trees. She wrote down the color of the apples on each tree.

red, red, yellow, green, red, green, red, red, yellow, red, green, green

First, organize the data. Then make a pictograph and a bar graph to show the data.

▶ **Model It** **You can organize the data in a tally chart.**

Red	Yellow	Green
HHT I	II	IIII

▶ **Model It** **You can organize the data in a table.**

Color of Apple	Number of Trees
Red	6
Yellow	2
Green	4

©Curriculum Associates, LLC   Copying is not permitted.

▶ **Connect It** **Make a pictograph and a bar graph.**

For Problems 9–11, use these graphs and the data
from the previous page.

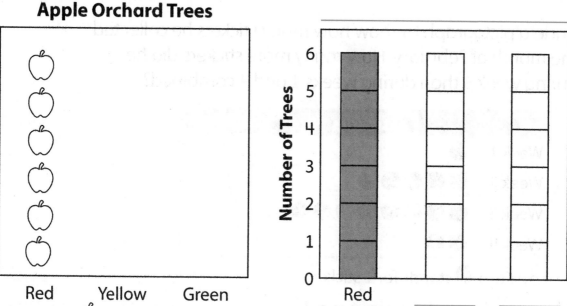

Apple Orchard Trees

Red   Yellow   Green

Key: Each 🍎 stands for
1 apple tree.

Number of Trees

6
5
4
3
2
1
0

Red

9 Complete the pictograph by drawing apples to show how many
yellow apple trees and green apple trees Lynn saw.

10 On the bar graph, fill in the title and labels.

11 Color the bar graph to show how many yellow apple
trees and green apple trees Lynn saw.

▶ **Try It** **Draw a pictograph and a bar graph.**

12 Make a pictograph and a bar graph for this data. Show your work
on a separate sheet of paper.

Favorite Colors			
Blue	**Purple**	**Green**	**Red**
5	6	2	3

Practice Making Bar Graphs and Pictographs

Study the model below. Then solve Problems 13–15.

Example

Gavin made a pictograph to show how many stickers he collected during the month of February. How many more stickers did he collect during week 3 than during weeks 1 and 4 combined?

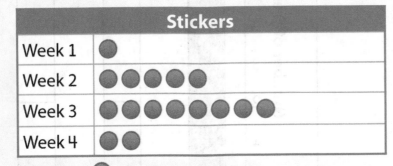

Key: Each ⬤ stands for 1 sticker.

Look at how you can show your work.

$$1 + 2 = 3 \qquad 8 - 3 = 5$$

Answer <u>He collected 5 more stickers during week 3 than</u>

<u>during weeks 1 and 4 combined.</u>

---

13 How many more stickers did Gavin collect during the last two weeks than during the first two weeks?

Show your work.

How many stickers did Gavin get during the last two weeks? How many stickers did he get during the first two weeks?

Answer _____

_____

14 Ally made this graph on Sunday morning. Then she read two more books that day. Fill in the graph to show that she read two more books on Sunday.

What is the total number of books for Sunday?

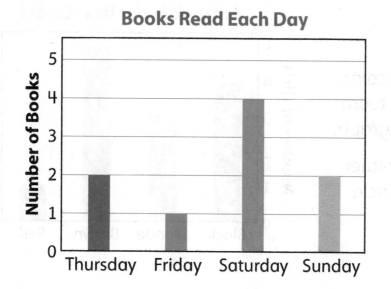

Books Read Each Day

Number of Books

Thursday   Friday   Saturday   Sunday

---

15 How many fewer books did Ally read on Thursday and Friday combined than on Saturday?

A 1

B 2

C 3

D 4

John chose **C** as the answer. This answer is wrong. How did John get his answer?

This problem has two steps. What do you need to do first?

_____

_____

Practice ⟩ **Making Bar Graphs and Pictographs**

Solve the problems.

Use the graph to solve Problems 1 and 2.

Maggie recorded the hair color of the girls on her softball team. She put her data in a bar graph.

Softball Team Hair Colors

1 How many girls have either brown or black hair? Circle the correct answer.

A 5

B 6

C 7

D 9

2 Circle *True* or *False* for each sentence.

a. There are more girls with black hair than brown hair.

True   False

b. There are more girls with brown hair than the other three colors combined.

True   False

c. There are two fewer girls with red hair than blonde hair.

True   False

d. There are eight girls with brown hair or blonde hair.

True   False

 ©Curriculum Associates, LLC   Copying is not permitted.

3 Wes recorded what he ate for breakfast for one week in the table at the right.

Complete the pictograph below using the data in the table. Draw a heart symbol to record each day in the table.

Day	Breakfast
Sun.	cereal
Mon.	cereal
Tues.	eggs
Wed.	eggs
Thur.	muffin
Fri.	eggs
Sat.	cereal

Breakfast Eaten	
Cereal	
_____	
Muffins	♡

Key: Each ♡ stands for 1 day.

4 Use your completed pictograph from Problem 3 to fill in the blanks below.

For breakfast, Wes had _____ for

3 days and _____ for 3 days.

Wes had cereal on _____ more days than

he had _____.

5 If Wes had eaten a muffin for breakfast on Saturday, how would the pictograph be different than it is now?

_____

_____

_____

✓ **Self Check** **Now you can make bar graphs and pictographs. Fill this in on the progress chart on page 153.**

Ⓖ Use What You Know

You know how to tell time to the hour and half hour.

Lucy started her piano lesson at the time shown on the clock.

What time does the clock show?

a. The short hand shows the hour. What number did the short hand just go past?

_____

b. The long hand shows the minutes. It is halfway around the clock. How many minutes are in a half hour?

_____

c. The time is halfway between which two hours?

_____ : _____ and _____ : _____

d. What time did Lucy start her piano lesson?

_____ : _____

  hours minutes

©Curriculum Associates, LLC   Copying is not permitted.

Look at the clock. The short hand is called the **hour hand**.
It tells you the **hour**.

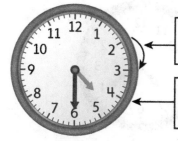

It takes 1 hour for the **hour hand** to
move from one number to the next.

Since the hour hand has gone past
the 4 (but isn't to the 5 yet), the hour is 4.

The long hand is called the **minute hand**.
It tells you the number of **minutes**.

It takes 5 minutes
for the **minute hand**
to move from one
number to the next.

The minute hand is pointing to
the **6**. Skip count by five **6** times
to find the number of minutes.
5, 10, 15, 20, 25, 30

When writing the time, write the hour, then a colon (:),
then the minutes. The clock shows 4:30.

▶ **Reflect** **Work with a partner.**

1 **Talk About It** Why can you skip count by five to show there
are 60 minutes in an hour?

Write About It _____

_____

_____

Learn About ▶ **Telling and Writing Time**

Read the problem. Then you will look at ways to tell and write time.

Evan started eating breakfast at the time shown on the clock.

What time does the clock show?

▶ **Picture It** **You can use the clock to find the hour and minutes.**

The hour hand is between the **7** and the **8**.

The minute hand is pointed at the **4**.
Skip count by five **4** times to find the minutes.

▶ **Picture It** **You can use a digital clock to show the time.**

The same time can be shown on a **digital clock**.
It shows the hour first, then the minutes.

A digital clock shows **AM** to mean "during the morning" or **PM** to mean "noon until midnight."

©Curriculum Associates, LLC   Copying is not permitted.

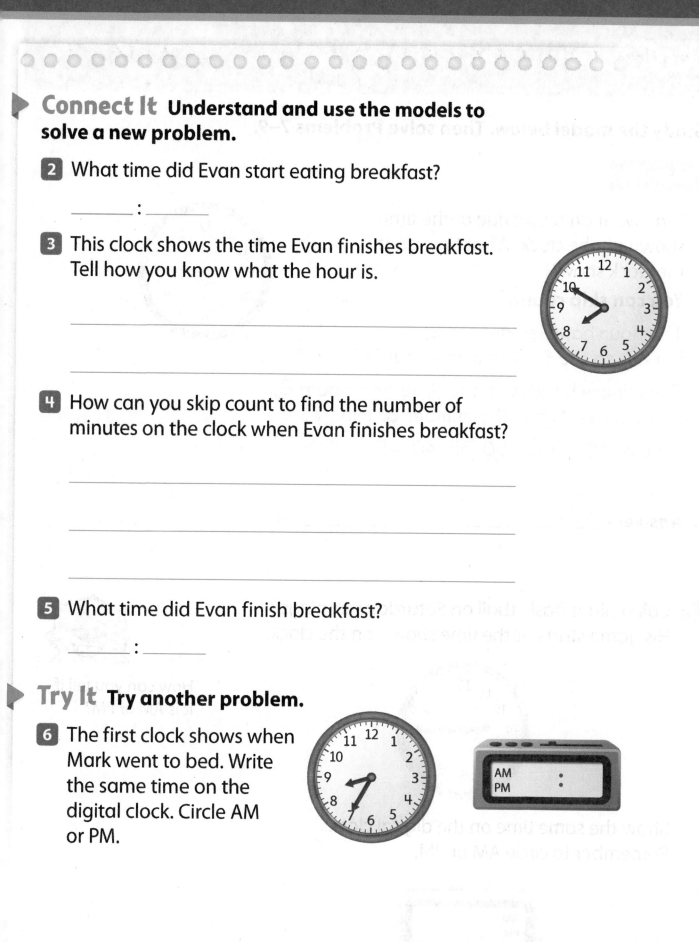

Connect It Understand and use the models to solve a new problem.

2 What time did Evan start eating breakfast?

_____ : _____

3 This clock shows the time Evan finishes breakfast. Tell how you know what the hour is.

_____

_____

4 How can you skip count to find the number of minutes on the clock when Evan finishes breakfast?

_____

_____

_____

5 What time did Evan finish breakfast?

_____ : _____

Try It Try another problem.

6 The first clock shows when Mark went to bed. Write the same time on the digital clock. Circle AM or PM.

AM
PM

Practice ▶ **Telling and Writing Time**

Study the model below. Then solve Problems 7–9.

Example

Dina went on a bike ride at the time shown on the clock. What time does the clock show?

You can skip count.

The hour hand is past the 2, but not to the 3 yet. So, the hour is 2.

The minute hand is on the 9, so skip count by five 9 times to find the number of minutes.

5, 10, 15, 20, 25, 30, 35, 40, 45

Answer _2:45_

7 Caleb plays basketball on Saturday mornings. His game starts at the time shown on the clock.

How can you tell if it is AM or PM?

Show the same time on the digital clock. Remember to circle AM or PM.

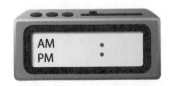

AM
PM

©Curriculum Associates, LLC Copying is not permitted.

8 Sophia had a meeting at the time shown on the digital clock below.
Show the same time on the other clock.

What two numbers will the hour hand be between? What number will the minute hand point to?

PM **1:40**

---

9 Jane got home from school at the time shown on the clock. What time did Jane get home?

A 5:15

B 3:05

C 3:25

D 4:25

Which hand tells the hour?

Emily chose **B** as the answer. This answer is wrong. How did Emily get her answer?

_____

_____

_____

_____

Practice ▸ **Telling and Writing Time**

Solve the problems.

1 Elsa went to swim practice after school. She finished at 5:45. Which clock shows the time Elsa finished? Circle all the correct answers.

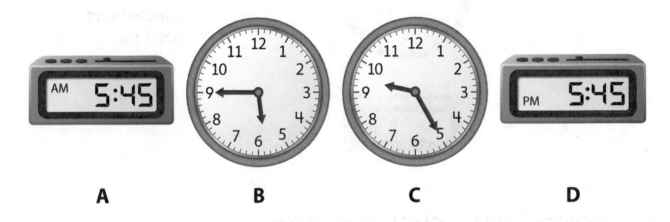

| A | B | C | D |

2 Where does the hour hand point when a clock shows 10:30? Circle the correct answer.

A at the 6

B at the 10

C between the 9 and the 10

D between the 10 and the 11

3 The minute hand on a clock points at the 10. What time could it be? Circle all the correct answers.

A 10:10

B 4:50

C 10:30

D 8:50

©Curriculum Associates, LLC Copying is not permitted.

4 Dylan finished his afternoon soccer practice at the time shown on the clock at the right.

Which clock below shows the time Dylan finished soccer practice? Circle the correct answer.

    A   **B**   **C**   **D**

5 Robin read until 7:35 in the evening. Draw hands on the clock to show that time. Then write the same time on the digital clock. Be sure to circle AM or PM.

6 The clock at the right is missing the minute hand. It is either 6:05 or 6:55. Which is correct? Explain how the hour hand can help you know the answer.

_____

_____

_____

_____

✓ **Self Check** **Now you can read and write time.**
Fill this in on the progress chart on page 153.

©Curriculum Associates, LLC   Copying is not permitted.

Ⓖ Use What You Know

You know how to count by ones, fives, and tens.

Lee, Seth, and Jack each have five coins.

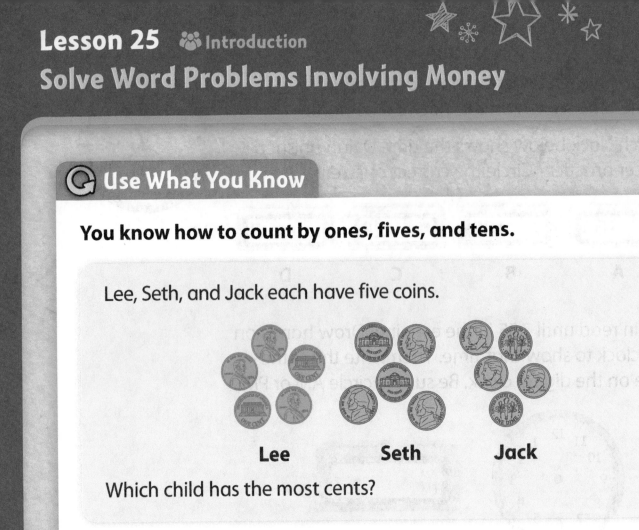

Lee   **Seth**   **Jack**

Which child has the most cents?

a. Lee has five pennies. Each penny is worth 1 cent. Count by ones to find how many cents she has.

_1_ , _2_ , ___ , ___ , ___

b. Seth has five nickels. Each nickel is worth 5 cents. Count by fives to find how many cents he has.

_5_ , _10_ , ___ , ___ , ___

c. Jack has five dimes. Each dime is worth 10 cents. Count by tens to find how many cents he has.

_10_ , _20_ , ___ , ___ , ___

d. Who has the most cents? Explain how you know.

_____

_____

©Curriculum Associates, LLC   Copying is not permitted.

▷▷ Find Out More

You can learn about the value of money.

Each type of coin and bill has a different value.

Name	Value	Front	Back
penny	1¢		
nickel	5¢		
dime	10¢		
quarter	25¢		many different kinds

We use ¢ to show cents and $ to show dollars. 5¢ is five cents. $5 is five dollars.

A $1 bill is worth the same amount as 100¢.

There are also other types of bills, such as $5, $10, $20, $50, and $100.

Reflect Work with a partner.

1 **Talk About It** Each child in the problem on the previous page has five coins. Why don't they all have the same amount of money?

Write About It _____

_____

_____

Learn About ▸ **Finding the Value of Coins**

Read the problem. Then you will explore ways to find the value of the coins.

Erik found some coins on the floor. How many cents did he find?

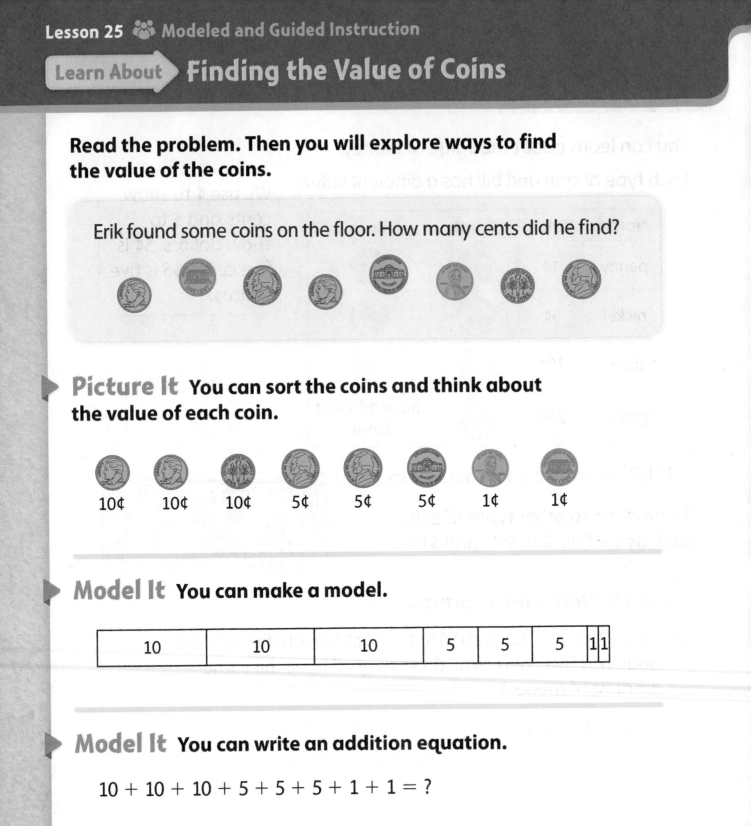

▸ **Picture It** **You can sort the coins and think about the value of each coin.**

10¢   10¢   10¢   5¢   5¢   5¢   1¢   1¢

▸ **Model It** **You can make a model.**

| 10 | 10 | 10 | 5 | 5 | 5 | 1 | 1 |

▸ **Model It** **You can write an addition equation.**

$10 + 10 + 10 + 5 + 5 + 5 + 1 + 1 = ?$

   ©Curriculum Associates, LLC   Copying is not permitted.

▶ Connect It Use skip counting and addition to find the value of the coins.

2 Use skip counting to find the value. Each time the coins change, be sure to change what you are counting by.

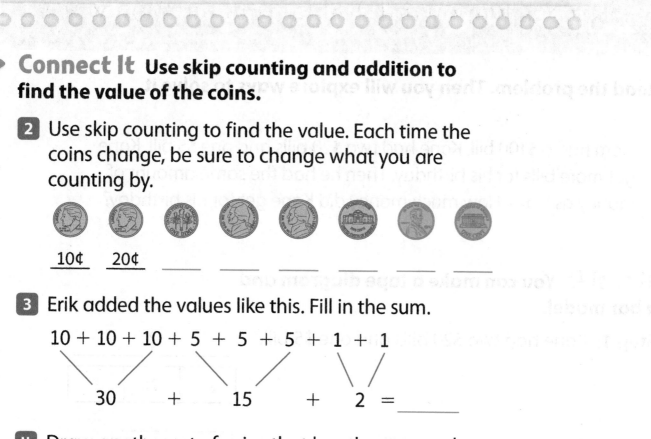

10¢   20¢   ____   ____   ____   ____   ____   ____

3 Erik added the values like this. Fill in the sum.

10 + 10 + 10 + 5 + 5 + 5 + 1 + 1

30   +   15   +   2 = _____

4 Draw another set of coins that has the same value as Erik's set of coins.

▶ Try It Try another problem.

5 Blaire has these coins.

How many cents does she have? _____ ¢

Draw another set of coins that is worth the same amount.

©Curriculum Associates, LLC   Copying is not permitted.

Learn About Solving Word Problems About Money

Read the problem. Then you will explore ways to solve it.

> Liam had a $100 bill. Kane had two $20 bills and one $5 bill. Kane got more bills for his birthday. Then he had the same amount of money as Liam. How much money did Kane get for his birthday?

▶ **Model It** **You can make a tape diagram and a bar model.**

Step 1: Kane had two $20 bills and one $5 bill.

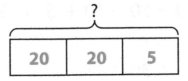

Step 2: Kane got some more bills. Then he had $100.

100	
45	?

▶ **Model It** **You can use open number lines.**

Step 1: Kane had two $20 bills and one $5 bill.

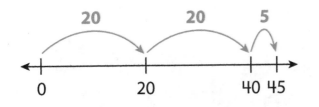

Step 2: Kane got some more bills. Then he had $100.

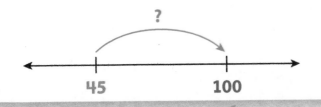

©Curriculum Associates, LLC Copying is not permitted.

▶ **Connect It** **Use the models to solve the problem.**

6 What do you find in Step 1?

_____

7 Write an addition equation for Step 1.

_____ + _____ + _____ = _____

8 How much money did Kane have after his birthday?
How do you know?

_____

_____

9 What do you find in Step 2?

_____

10 Write a subtraction equation for Step 2.

_____ − _____ = _____

11 How much money did Kane get for his birthday? _____
Draw a set of bills that he could have received.

▶ **Try It** **Try another problem.**

12 Izzy has two $10 bills and three $5 bills. Matt has two $5 bills and a
$20 bill. Who has more money? How much more? Show your work.

_____

_____

Practice > **Solving Word Problems About Money**

Study the model below. Then solve Problems 13–15.

Example

Paige has two quarters, one dime, and one nickel. Andre has six dimes. Which set of coins is worth more? How much more?

You can show your work with models.

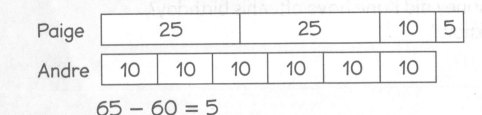

Paige	25	25	10	5

Andre	10	10	10	10	10	10

$$65 - 60 = 5$$

Answer Paige's set of coins is worth 5¢ more than Andre's.

---

13 Anthony has $25 in bills. Name two ways he could have $25.

Show your work.

Think about ways you could use $1, $5, $10, and $20 bills to add up to $25.

Answer _____

_____

©Curriculum Associates, LLC   Copying is not permitted.

14 A pen costs 35¢. Logan paid with two quarters.
What coins could Logan get back as change?

Show your work.

What are two
quarters worth?
How do you figure
out the change
Logan should get?

Answer _____

---

15 Johanna has these coins in her pocket.

How much are the coins worth?

A 8¢

B 40¢

C 80¢

D $2

Try skip counting to
find the total.

Mary chose **C** as the answer. This answer is wrong.
How did Mary get her answer?

_____

_____

Practice ⟩ **Solving Word Problems About Money**

Solve the problems.

1 What is the total value of these coins?
Circle the correct answer.

A 52¢   **C** 67¢

B 62¢   **D** 77¢

2 A bookmark costs 68¢. Haley uses 3 quarters to pay
for it. Which coins should she get back in change?
Circle the correct answer.

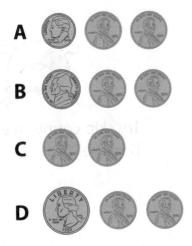

A

B

C

D

3 Circle *True* or *False* for each statement.

	True	False
a. A dime is worth the same as ten pennies.	True	False
b. A nickel is worth the same as two dimes.	True	False
c. A quarter is worth the same as five nickels.	True	False
d. A quarter is worth the same as two dimes and one nickel.	True	False

   ©Curriculum Associates, LLC   Copying is not permitted.

4 Which set of coins is worth 31¢?
Circle all the correct answers.

A

B

C

D

5 Tess has more than three bills. They have a total value of $30. What bills could Tess have?

Show your work.

_____

_____

6 Jim answers Problem 5. He says Tess could have four $10 bills. Do you agree? Explain why or why not.

_____

_____

_____

✔ Self Check   **Now you can solve problems using money.**
Fill this in on the progress chart on page 153.

Study an Example Problem and Solution

**Read this problem about measuring in centimeters.
Then look at Bella's solution to the problem.**

Buttons

Bella saves buttons to decorate things she makes.
Bella wants to glue some buttons on the front of
a pencil box. Each button is the same width.

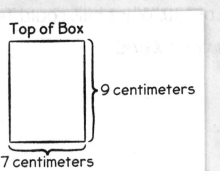

- Put buttons in a line around all 4 edges.
- The buttons do not have to touch.
- Measure the button to help you plan.

Top of Box

9 centimeters

7 centimeters

How can Bella decorate the pencil box? Draw a
picture. Tell how many buttons she needs.

Show how Bella's solution matches the checklist.

✏️ Problem-Solving Checklist

☐ Tell what is known.
☐ Tell what the problem is asking.
☐ Show all your work.
☐ Show that the solution works.

a. Circle something that is known.

b. Underline something that you need to find.

c. Draw a box around what you do to solve the problem.

d. Put a checkmark next to the part that shows the solution works.

©Curriculum Associates, LLC   Copying is not permitted.

Hi, I'm Bella. Here's how I solved this problem.

Bella's Solution

▷ **First, I can measure the button.**

It is 1 centimeter wide.

▷ **I need 4 lines of buttons.**

I'll put 1 centimeter of space between the buttons.

▷ **I can make a drawing to show my thinking.**

- Start with the long sides.
- Draw and count 9 centimeters.
- Then make the top and bottom numbers.
- Draw and count 7 centimeters.

I made a drawing to help me solve the problem.

I checked my work by adding.

Both sides have 5 buttons and 4 spaces. 5 + 4 = 9

The bottom and top each have 4 buttons and 3 spaces. 4 + 3 = 7

9 centimeters and 7 centimeters match the drawing.

▷ **I can count all the buttons to see how many I need.**

There are 14 buttons.

Try **Another Approach**

There are many ways to solve problems. Think about how you might solve the Buttons problem in a different way.

Buttons

Bella saves buttons to decorate things she makes. Bella wants to glue some buttons on the front of a pencil box. Each button is the same width.

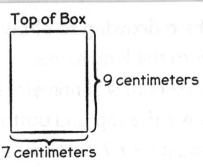

- Put buttons in a line around all 4 edges.
- The buttons do not have to touch.
- Measure the button to help you plan.

Top of Box

9 centimeters

7 centimeters

How can Bella decorate the pencil box? Draw a picture. Tell how many buttons she needs.

▶ **Plan It** **Answer this question to help you start thinking about a plan.**

The example answer has spaces between each button. How could you make a design with no space between the buttons?

_____

_____

_____

©Curriculum Associates, LLC   Copying is not permitted.

Solve It Find a different solution for the Buttons problem. Show all your work on a separate sheet of paper.

You may want to use the problem-solving tips to get started.

Problem-Solving Tips

- **Tools**

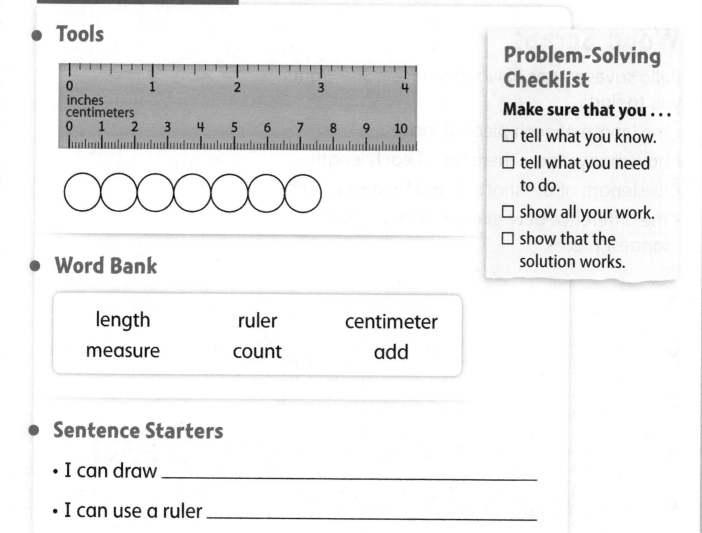

Problem-Solving Checklist

Make sure that you . . .

☐ tell what you know.

☐ tell what you need to do.

☐ show all your work.

☐ show that the solution works.

- **Word Bank**

length	ruler	centimeter
measure	count	add

- **Sentence Starters**

• I can draw _____

• I can use a ruler _____

Reflect

Use Mathematical Practices Talk about this question with a partner.

• **Persevere** What can you do if you get to a difficult part of the problem?

Discuss ▸ **Models and Strategies**

Solve the problem on a separate sheet of paper.
There are different ways you can solve it.

Wood Scraps

Bella saves scraps of wood to reuse. She wants
you to find:

• the length of each piece in inches.

• how many pieces there are of each length.

• the length of the shortest and longest pieces.

• the difference between the shortest and
longest pieces.

a

b

c

d

e

f

g

h

How can Bella organize the data?

©Curriculum Associates, LLC Copying is not permitted.

▶ Plan It and Solve It Find a solution to Bella's Wood Scraps problem.

Make sure to do all parts of the task.

- Measure each piece of wood.
- Organize the data in a line plot or bar graph.
- Use words to describe the lengths of the scraps of wood.

You may want to use the problem-solving tips to get started.

Problem-Solving Tips

- **Questions**
  - What tool should I use to measure?
  - How will I show the data?

- **Word Bank**

length	longer	shorter
difference	inches	longest
shortest	compare	

- **Sentence Starters**
  - The length of _____
  - The longest piece _____

Problem-Solving Checklist

Make sure that you . . .
- ☐ tell what you know.
- ☐ tell what you need to do.
- ☐ show all your work.
- ☐ show that the solution works.

▶ Reflect

Use Mathematical Practices Talk about this question with a partner.

- **Use Tools** How can you decide what measuring tool to use?

Solve the problem on a separate sheet of paper.

Craft Supplies

Bella likes to recycle items for her projects. But she
still has to buy some things. Bella wants to buy
some wooden hearts and some wooden letters.
She can spend up to $1 on hearts and
up to $1 on letters.

Wooden hearts: 44¢ each

Wooden letters: 28¢ each

How many hearts and letters can Bella buy?

▶ **Solve It** **Help Bella decide what to buy.**

- Tell how many hearts and letters to buy.
- Give the cost for the hearts and for the letters.
- Name a group of coins she could use to buy hearts.
- Name a group of coins she could use to buy letters.

▶ **Reflect**

Use Mathematical Practices Talk about this question
with a partner.

- **Use Structure** How did you use the values of coins
  to solve the problem?

©Curriculum Associates, LLC   Copying is not permitted.

Bella's Bottles

Bella wants to make a garden border.

She will use red and blue recycled bottles to make it.

Read Bella's notes.

My Notes

- The whole border is between 60 and 72 inches.
- Part A is between 45 and 55 inches.
- Part B is between 15 and 25 inches.

Garden

Part A	Part B
Red Bottles	Blue Bottles

How can Bella design her border?

▶ **Solve It** **Help Bella make a plan for her border.**

- Write the length for each part.
- Show all your work.
- Tell why your measurements work.

▶ **Reflect**

Use Mathematical Practices Talk about this question with a partner.

- **Make an Argument** How did you show that your measurements work?

©Curriculum Associates, LLC   Copying is not permitted.

Solve the problems.

1 Stephanie buys a pen that costs 57¢. She pays with 3 quarters. Complete the table to show different ways she could get her change.

Dimes	Nickles	Pennies
0		
0		
	0	
	0	

2 Juan counts the paper shapes he has.

- He counts 7 hearts.
- He counts 3 fewer stars than hearts.
- He counts 16 paper shapes in all.

Complete the pictograph to show the paper shapes Juan has.

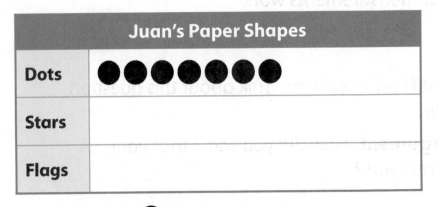

Key: Each ⬤ stands for 1 paper shape.

©Curriculum Associates, LLC   Copying is not permitted.

3 Catelyn has a rope that is 66 inches long. She cuts it into two pieces. Circle *Yes* or *No* to tell whether each pair of lengths below could be the lengths of the pieces.

a. 44 inches and 24 inches   Yes   No

b. 40 inches and 26 inches   Yes   No

c. 35 inches and 32 inches   Yes   No

d. 33 inches and 33 inches   Yes   No

4 The hour hand fell off this clock. Circle *Yes* or *No* to tell if each time shown below could be the time shown on the clock.

a. 3:25   Yes   No

b. 4:05   Yes   No

c. 5:25   Yes   No

d. 6:20   Yes   No

4 Alec asked his friends to name their favorite sport. Then he made this bar graph.

How many more friends chose soccer and football than baseball and tennis? Circle the correct answer.

A 6

B 7

C 13

D 20

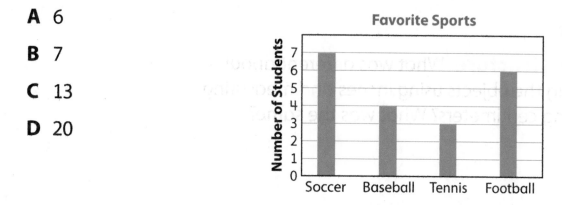

Favorite Sports

Performance Task

Answer the questions. Show all your work on separate paper.

Measure 5 objects in inches and in centimeters. Make a table like the one below. Write the names of the objects and the lengths in the table.

Checklist

Did You . . .

☐ measure each object using both units?

☐ check your answers?

☐ explain your answers?

Object	Length in Inches	Length in Centimeters

- What is the total length of all the objects in inches? What is the total length in centimeters?

- Compare the total lengths. Is there a greater number of centimeters or inches? Explain why.

- Use your measurements to make a line plot like the one below. The line plot can show inches or centimeters.

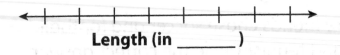

Length (in _____)

Reflect

Look for Structure What was different about measuring the objects using inches and measuring them using centimeters? What was the same?

 ©Curriculum Associates, LLC Copying is not permitted.

Unit 4
Geometry

Let's learn about naming shapes, breaking them apart, and putting them together.

Real-World Connection Look around your classroom. How many shapes can you name? Do you see shapes that you don't know the names of? Can you describe the parts of shapes? Some shapes have straight sides, and some shapes have curves. Some shapes have sides that are all the same length. Others have sides that are different lengths.

In This Unit You will learn the names of shapes and how to describe their parts. You will put shapes together to make new shapes. You will also divide shapes into equal parts.

✔ **Self Check**

Before starting this unit, check off the skills you know below.

I can:	Before this unit	After this unit
recognize and draw different shapes.	☐	☐
break up a rectangle into squares.	☐	☐
divide shapes into equal parts.	☐	☐

Recognize and Draw Shapes

Use What You Know

Find circles, triangles, squares, and rectangles.

Macy makes this collage with cutout shapes. How many circles, triangles, squares, and rectangles does she use?

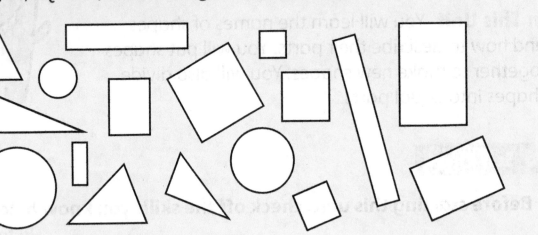

Color the shapes as described below.
Then write how many there are of each shape.

a. Color the circles red. _____ circles

b. Color the triangles blue. _____ triangles

c. Color the squares yellow. _____ squares

d. Color the rectangles green. _____ rectangles

©Curriculum Associates, LLC   Copying is not permitted.

Most shapes have sides and angles.

Triangles have 3 sides and 3 angles.

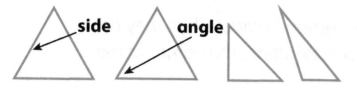

Quadrilaterals have 4 sides and 4 angles.

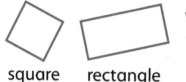

square   rectangle   trapezoid rhombus

Pentagons have 5 sides and 5 angles.

Hexagons have 6 sides and 6 angles.

Reflect **Work with a partner.**

1 **Talk About It** Look at the hexagons above. Can the shape at the right be called a hexagon? Explain.

Write About It _____

_____

_____

Learn About Naming and Drawing Shapes

Read the problem. Then you will explore sides and angles of shapes.

Some friends hunt for shapes around school. Then they draw pictures of the objects they see. What are the names of the shapes that they draw?

▶ **Picture It** **You can look for shapes.**

▶ **Draw It** **You can draw the shapes.**

Shape A   Shape B   Shape C

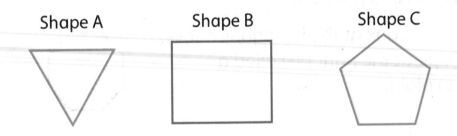

©Curriculum Associates, LLC   Copying is not permitted.

► **Connect It** **Use the number of sides and angles to name shapes.**

2 Look at *Draw It* to complete the chart below.

Shape	Shape Name	Number of Sides	Number of Angles
A			
B			
C			

3 What do you notice about the number of sides and the number of angles in each shape?

_____

_____

4 What is another name for Shape B? Explain.

_____

_____

► **Try It** **Try another problem.**

5 Draw 3 shapes. One has 3 angles. One has 4 angles. One has 5 sides. Make the shapes different from those in *Draw It*.

Learn About ▶ **Making Shapes**

Read the problem. Then explore different ways to make a hexagon.

Meg has these shapes. How can she put them together to make a hexagon?

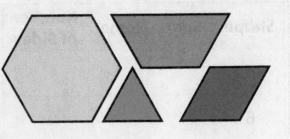

Model It You can make the hexagon with the same shapes.

Both parts of the hexagon are the same shape.

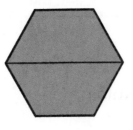

Model It You can make the hexagon with different shapes.

Some parts are the same shape but some are different.

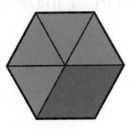

©Curriculum Associates, LLC   Copying is not permitted.

Connect It Name shapes that make a hexagon.

6 Look at the first *Model It*. What shapes make up the hexagon? How many of each shape?

_____

7 Look at the second *Model It*. What shapes make up the hexagon? How many of each shape?

_____

8 Find two new ways to make a hexagon. Use the shapes at the top of the previous page. Make a drawing to show each way. Then write how many of each shape make up each hexagon.

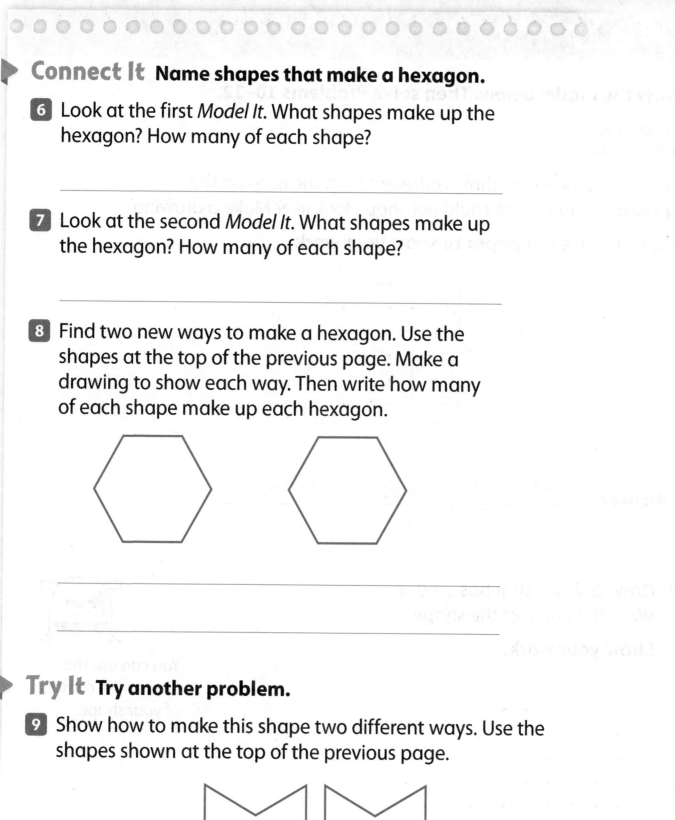

_____

Try It Try another problem.

9 Show how to make this shape two different ways. Use the shapes shown at the top of the previous page.

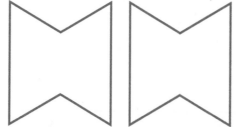

Practice ▶ **Recognizing and Drawing Shapes**

Study the model below. Then solve Problems 10–12.

Example

Lin drew a hexagon that is different from the ones on the previous page. What could her shape look like? Make a drawing.

You can use dot paper to show your work.

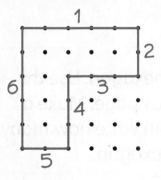

Answer _This shape has 6 sides. It is a hexagon._

---

10 Draw a shape that has 5 sides.
Write the name of the shape.

Show your work.

You can use the dots as the corners of your shape.

Answer _____

©Curriculum Associates, LLC   Copying is not permitted.

11 Solve the riddle.

I have fewer sides than a pentagon.

I am not a quadrilateral.

What am I?

Show your work.

> What shapes have fewer sides than a pentagon?

Answer _____

---

12 Which statement is true?

A Rectangles are not quadrilaterals.

B Quadrilaterals can have 5 angles.

C All quadrilaterals have 4 sides.

D All quadrilaterals have 4 equal sides.

> Make a picture of all the different quadrilaterals you know.

Alma chose **D** as the answer. This answer is wrong. How did Alma get her answer?

_____

_____

_____

_____

Practice ▶ **Recognizing and Drawing Shapes**

Solve the problems.

1 Fill in the blanks. Use the words in the box.

  a. _____ triangles have 3 sides.

  b. _____ triangles have sides the same length.

  c. _____ triangles have 4 angles.

> Some
>
> No
>
> All

2 Ross draws a shape with 6 angles. What is true about his shape? Circle all the correct answers.

  A It is a pentagon.

  B It has 6 sides.

  C It has 5 sides.

  D It is a hexagon.

3 What is true about the shape below?
Circle all the correct answers.

  A It is a pentagon.

  B It is a quadrilateral.

  C It can be made up of 2 trapezoids.

  D It has 3 angles.

 ©Curriculum Associates, LLC   Copying is not permitted.

Use the shape in the box for Problems 4 and 5.

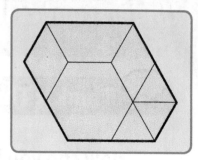

4 What is the name of the big shape that is made by putting all the small shapes together? How do you know?

_____

_____

5 There are 7 smaller shapes that make up the big shape. How many are there of each smaller shape?

_____ triangles

_____ quadrilaterals

_____ hexagon

6 Draw a shape that has between 3 and 6 sides. Use the dots below. What is the name of your shape? Explain how you know.

· · · · · ·
· · · · · ·
· · · · · ·
· · · · · ·
· · · · · ·

_____

_____

_____

✓ **Self Check** **Now you can count sides and angles. Fill this in on the progress chart on page 247.**

Think It Through

How can you break up a rectangle into squares of the same size?

You know how to put shapes together to make bigger shapes. You can make a rectangle by using just squares.

Think **You can use squares that are the same size to make a rectangle.**

You can put 12 squares in 1 row to make a rectangle.

You can also put them in 2 rows to make a rectangle.
Each row has 6 squares.

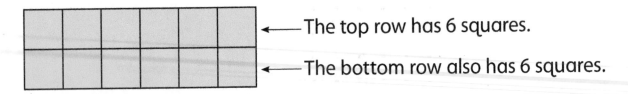
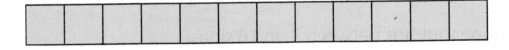

← The top row has 6 squares.

← The bottom row also has 6 squares.

✏️ Make a drawing of 12 squares. Put the squares in 3 rows.

✏️ There are _____ rows of squares.

There are _____ squares in each row.

Think Fill a rectangle with squares that are the same size.

Use graph paper to make this rectangle.

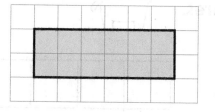

You can fill a rectangle with squares. All the squares must be the same size. All the shapes have to be squares.

Here are two ways to draw the rectangle using squares that are the same size.

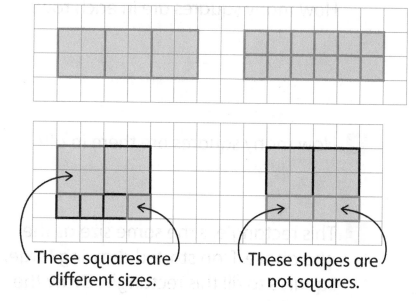

These rectangles are not drawn using squares that are the same size.

These squares are different sizes.

These shapes are not squares.

▶ Reflect Work with a partner.

1 Talk About It You have 9 squares that are the same size. Can you make a rectangle with the squares in 1 row? 2 rows? 3 rows?

Write About It _____

_____

_____

Think About Using Squares to Fill a Rectangle

🔍 **Let's Explore the Idea** Fill rectangles with squares. Then find the total number of squares.

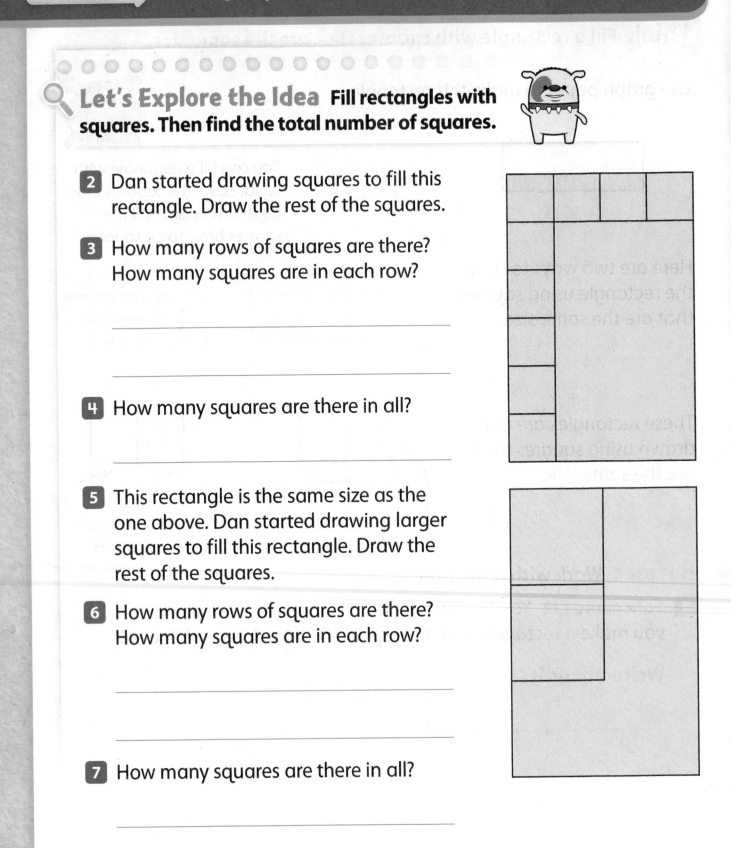

2 Dan started drawing squares to fill this rectangle. Draw the rest of the squares.

3 How many rows of squares are there? How many squares are in each row?

_____

_____

4 How many squares are there in all?

_____

5 This rectangle is the same size as the one above. Dan started drawing larger squares to fill this rectangle. Draw the rest of the squares.

6 How many rows of squares are there? How many squares are in each row?

_____

_____

7 How many squares are there in all?

_____

Let's Talk About It

Work with a partner.

8 How did you know how many squares were missing in the first rectangle?

_____

_____

9 How did you know how many squares were missing in the second rectangle?

_____

_____

10 The two rectangles are the same size. Why is there a different number of squares in each one?

_____

_____

▶ **Try It Another Way** **Use dot paper to draw squares in rectangles.**

11 Show two different ways to fill the rectangle with same-sized squares.

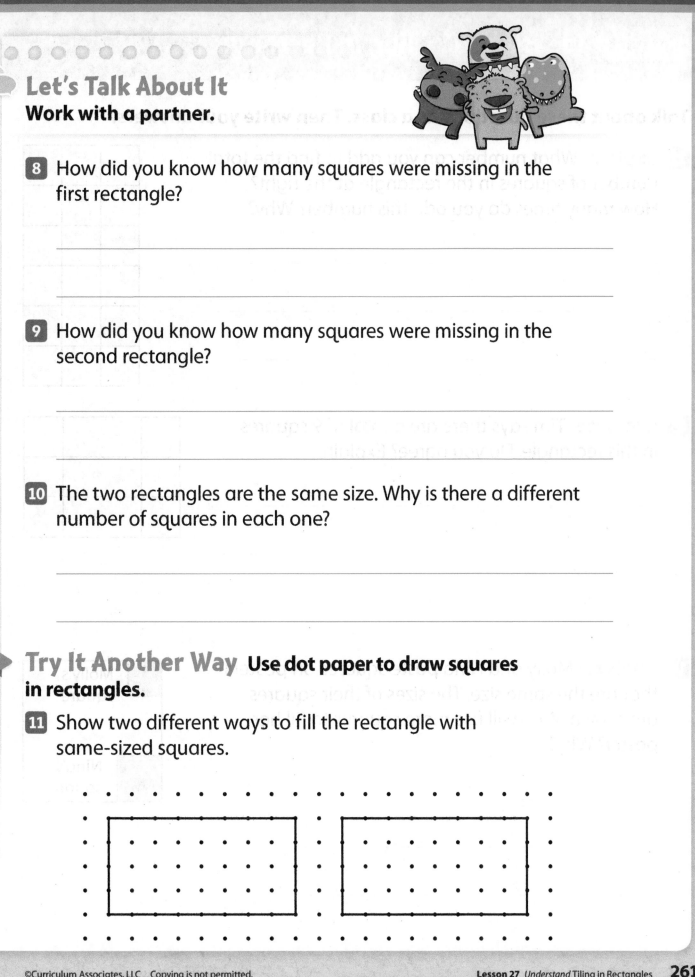

Connect ▶ **Ideas About Tiling in Rectangles**

Talk about these questions as a class. Then write your answers.

12 **Explain** What number can you add to find the total number of squares in the rectangle at the right? How many times do you add this number? Why?

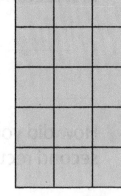

_____

_____

_____

13 **Evaluate** Tim says there are a total of 9 squares in this rectangle. Do you agree? Explain.

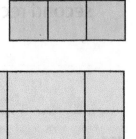

_____

_____

_____

14 **Analyze** Molly and Nina paste squares on posters that are the same size. The sizes of their squares are shown. Who will use more squares to fill her poster? Why?

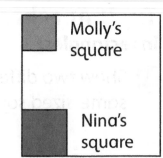

Molly's square

Nina's square

_____

_____

_____

©Curriculum Associates, LLC   Copying is not permitted.

Apply **Ideas About Tiling in Rectangles** 263

Put It Together **Use what you have learned to complete this task.**

15 Sue is making a mosaic design. She has squares that are the sizes below. But she can only use squares that are all the same size.

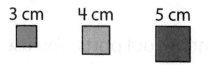

3 cm   4 cm   5 cm

Sue will use the squares to fill a piece of paper that is 24 centimeters long and 12 centimeters wide.

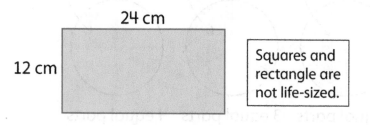

24 cm

12 cm

Squares and rectangle are not life-sized.

Part A Can Sue use the 3-centimeter squares to make her design? If so, how many squares will she need? Draw a picture at the right to help you explain.

_____

_____

Part B Repeat Part A for the 4-centimeter squares.

_____

_____

Part C Repeat Part A for the 5-centimeter squares.

_____

_____

Think It Through

How do you divide shapes into 2, 3, and 4 equal parts?

The circles are divided into equal parts. You use the number of equal parts to name the parts.

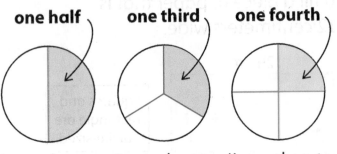

one half   one third   one fourth

2 equal parts   3 equal parts   4 equal parts

Think **Equal parts cover an equal amount of the shape.**

Think about sharing a sandwich with a friend.
You want each piece to be the same size.

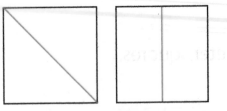   

These squares show equal parts. So each person gets the same amount.

In this square, one part is bigger than the other.

✏ Draw another way you could share a sandwich equally with a friend. Use the square at the right.

©Curriculum Associates, LLC   Copying is not permitted.

Think Equal parts can have different shapes.

These squares are all the same size. Each smaller shape covers one fourth of the square. So each smaller shape is an equal part of the square.

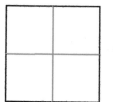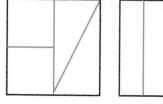

Think: Divide the square in half. Then divide each half in half.

These squares are the same size as the ones above. Each is divided into 3 equal parts, or thirds. So each smaller shape is an equal part of the square.

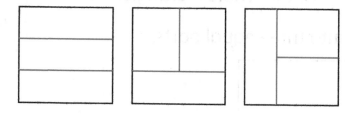

▶ Reflect Work with a partner.

1 Talk About It Draw two squares that are the same size as the ones above. Divide one into fourths and one into thirds in different ways than above. Which parts are bigger, the fourths or thirds? Explain.

Write About It _____

_____

_____

Think About ▶ **Dividing Rectangles into Equal Parts**

🔍 **Let's Explore the Idea** Follow the
directions for each rectangle.

2 Divide this rectangle into two equal parts.

3 Complete this sentence about the rectangle in
Problem 2. Use a word from the box at the right.

Each part is a _____ of the whole rectangle.

half
third
fourth

4 Divide this rectangle into three equal parts.

5 Complete this sentence about the rectangle in
Problem 4. Use a word from the box at the right.

Each part is a _____ of the whole rectangle.

half
third
fourth

6 Divide this rectangle into four equal parts.

7 Complete this sentence about the rectangle in
Problem 6. Use a word from the box at the right.

Each part is a _____ of the whole rectangle.

half
third
fourth

©Curriculum Associates, LLC Copying is not permitted.

Let's Talk About It
Work with a partner.

8 How many halves are in the big rectangle in Problem 2?

_____

9 How many thirds are in the big rectangle in Problem 4?

_____

10 How many fourths are in the big rectangle in Problem 6?

_____

▶ Try It Another Way Show a different way to make halves, thirds, and fourths.

11 Show another way to divide a rectangle into halves.

12 Show another way to divide a rectangle into thirds.

13 Show another way to divide a rectangle into fourths.

©Curriculum Associates, LLC   Copying is not permitted.

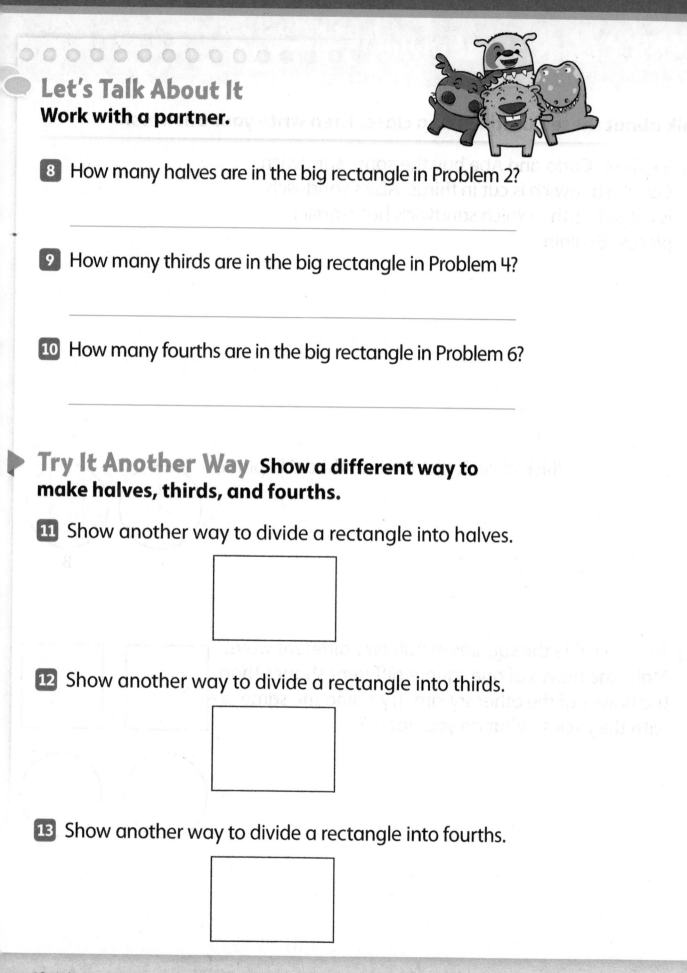

Connect ▶ **Ideas About Dividing into Parts**

Talk about these questions as a class. Then write your answers.

14 **Explain** Carlo and Abe buy the same sandwich. Carlo's sandwich is cut in thirds. Abe's sandwich is cut in fourths. Which sandwich has smaller pieces? Explain.

_____

_____

_____

_____

15 **Compare** Which circle is divided into thirds? Explain.

_____

_____

_____

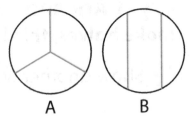

A   B

16 **Draw** Divide the squares in half two different ways. Make the halves of one square different shapes than the halves of the other square. Try doing the same with the circles. What do you notice?

_____

_____

_____

©Curriculum Associates, LLC   Copying is not permitted.

Apply ▶ **Ideas About Dividing into Parts**   269

Put It Together **Use what you have learned to complete this task.**

17 Shara and her mom make these 3 pizzas for a party.

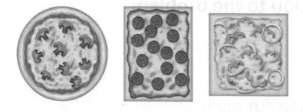

Part A Shara will have 10 people at the party. Draw how she could cut each pizza so every person gets 1 piece of pizza.

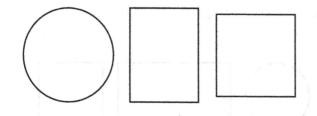

Part B Shara asks more people to the party. Now there will be 12 people. Draw how she could cut each pizza so every person gets 1 piece of pizza.

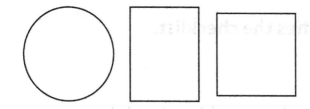

Part C Do you think each person gets an equal amount of pizza? Explain.

_____

_____

_____

©Curriculum Associates, LLC   Copying is not permitted.

MP1 Make sense
of problems and
persevere in
solving them.

Recognize and Use Shapes

Study an Example Problem and Solution

Read this problem about breaking shapes into equal parts. Then look at Luna's solution to the problem.

Cake Shapes

Luna makes 3 cakes. She wants to cut each cake into equal-size pieces. Read Luna's notes.

My Notes

My cakes are in the shape of a circle, a rectangle, and a square.

- Cut one cake into halves.
- Cut one into thirds.
- Cut one into fourths.

Show one way Luna can cut the cakes.

Show how Luna's solution matches the checklist.

✏️ Problem-Solving Checklist

- ☐ Tell what is known.
- ☐ Tell what the problem is asking.
- ☐ Show all your work.
- ☐ Show that the solution works.

a. **Circle** something that is known.

b. **Underline** something that you need to find.

c. **Draw a box around** what you do to solve the problem.

d. **Put a checkmark** next to the part that shows the solution works.

©Curriculum Associates, LLC Copying is not permitted.

Luna's Solution

▷ **I know what** halves, thirds, and fourths are.

Halves are 2 equal parts.

Thirds are 3 equal parts.

Fourths are 4 equal parts.

I thought about what I already know.

▷ **I need to cut** each shape into a different number of equal parts.

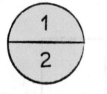

2 half-circles
(2 halves)

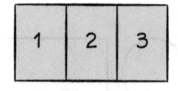

3 same-size rectangles
(3 thirds)

4 same-size triangles
(4 fourths)

▷ **I can tell how I cut the cakes.**

I cut the circle cake in halves.

I cut the rectangle cake in thirds.

I cut the square cake in fourths.

I labeled the pictures to check my thinking.

Try ▶ Another Approach

There are many ways to solve problems. Think about how to solve the Cake Shapes problem in a different way.

Cake Shapes

Luna makes 3 cakes. She wants to cut each cake into equal-size pieces. Read Luna's notes.

My Notes

My cakes are in the shape of a circle, a rectangle, and a square.

- Cut one cake into halves.
- Cut one into thirds.
- Cut one into fourths.

Show one way Luna can cut the cakes.

Plan It Answer this question to help you start thinking about a plan.

Look at the sample answer. How can you cut each shape into a different number of pieces?

_____

_____

_____

_____

_____

  ©Curriculum Associates, LLC   Copying is not permitted.

Solve It Find a different solution for the Cake Shapes problem. Show all your work on a separate sheet of paper.

You may want to use the problem-solving tips to get started.

Problem-Solving Tips

- **Questions**

  - Can I make pieces that are triangles?
  - Can I make pieces that are rectangles?
  - Can I cut a circle into 3 equal parts? 4 equal parts?

- **Word Bank**

equal	a half	halves	square
shape	a third	thirds	rectangle
	a fourth	fourths	circle

- **Sentence Starters**

  - There are _____ equal parts.

  - This shape is cut into _____

Problem-Solving Checklist

Make sure that you . . .

☐ tell what you know.

☐ tell what you need to do.

☐ show all your work.

☐ show that the solution works.

Reflect

Use Mathematical Practices Talk about this question with a partner.

- **Use Structure** How can you use the name of the fraction to tell how many equal parts it describes?

Discuss ▶ **Models and Strategies**

Solve the problem on a separate sheet of paper.
There are different ways you can solve it.

Cutting Cakes

Luna's friends make cakes in all shapes and sizes.
Luna helps them plan ways to cut the cakes into
pieces of different sizes. Here is one plan.

My Cake Cutting Plan
- Draw squares on the top of the cake
  to show how to cut it into pieces.
- Each square must be the same size.

Luna has a square cake like this one.
Each side is 6 inches long.

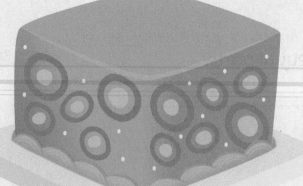

What size squares can Luna cut the cake into?

   ©Curriculum Associates, LLC   Copying is not permitted.

▶ Plan It and Solve It Find a solution for Luna's Cake Cutting problem.

Use the diagram of Luna's square cake on the Cutting Cakes Activity Sheet.

• Divide the square into same-size smaller squares.
• Then write the length of the sides of your squares.
• Last, tell why the pieces work with Luna's plan.

You may want to use the problem-solving tips to get started.

Problem-Solving Tips

● **Questions**

  • Can I use squares that have 1-inch sides? 2-inch sides? 4-inch sides?

● **Tools**

● **Word Bank**

square	sides	equal
inches	size	

Problem-Solving Checklist

Make sure that you . . .

☐ tell what you know.
☐ tell what you need to do.
☐ show all your work.
☐ show that the solution works.

▶ Reflect

Use Mathematical Practices Talk about this question with a partner.

• **Use Tools** How can you put the square tiles together to make different-size squares?

Solve the problem on a separate sheet of paper.

Create a Cake 1

Luna wants to make a cake that looks like this fish.

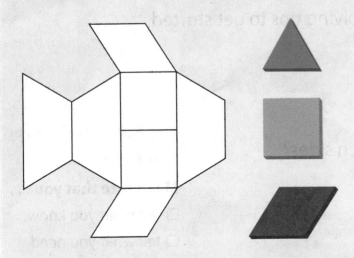

How can Luna make the cake with the shapes shown?

▷ **Solve It Help Luna make the cake shown above.**

Use the Create a Cake 1 Activity Sheet and the
shapes shown above.
- Find a way to use Luna's pieces to make the fish.
- Draw outlines of the shapes you used.
- Make a list of the shapes that you used.
- Tell how many of each shape you used.

▷ **Reflect**

Use Mathematical Practices Talk about this question
with a partner.

- **Make an Argument** How do you know that you named
each shape correctly?

©Curriculum Associates, LLC   Copying is not permitted.

Create a Cake 2

Luna needs to make a cake in this design.

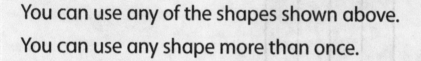

You can use any of the shapes shown above.

You can use any shape more than once.

▷ **Solve It** **Help Luna make the cake shown above.**

Use the Create a Cake 2 Activity Sheet and the
shapes shown above.
• Find two different ways to make the design.
• Draw outlines of the shapes you used.
• Make a list of the shapes that you used.
• Tell how many of each shape you used.

▷ **Reflect**

Use Mathematical Practices Talk about this question
with a partner.

• **Use Tools** How did you use the pattern block shapes to
help you solve this problem?

Solve the problems.

1 Kate has 18 square tiles. How can she arrange them to make a rectangle? Circle all the correct answers.

   A 10 rows of 8 squares

   B 9 rows of 2 squares

   C 6 rows of 3 squares

   D 5 rows of 4 squares

2 Meg drew this rectangle and divided it into four equal parts.

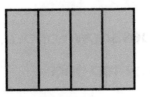

Which rectangle below is divided into parts that are the same size as the parts in Meg's rectangle? Circle all the correct answers.

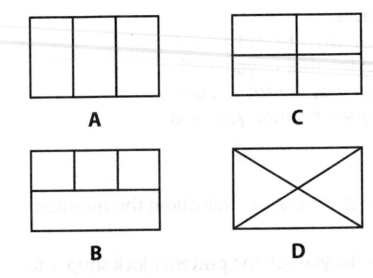

        A   **C**

        B   **D**

©Curriculum Associates, LLC   Copying is not permitted.

3 Dennis drew a hexagon. Circle *True* or *False* for each statement below about the shape Dennis drew.

    a. It has 6 angles.   True   False

    b. It is a quadrilateral.   True   False

    c. It has more than 5 sides.   True   False

    d. It has fewer angles than a rectangle.   True   False

4 Draw the rest of the squares to fill this rectangle.
Make all your squares the same size as the gray square.

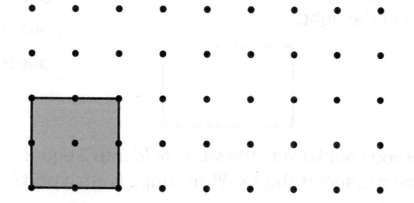

How many squares are there in all?

Answer _____ squares

5 Scott says that one third of this circle is shaded.
Do you agree? Explain why or why not.

_____

_____

Performance Task

Answer the questions. Use the shapes on this page. Show the rest of your work on separate paper.

Keeth Elementary School is having Field Day. Each grade plays on a separate field.

Checklist

Did You . . .

☐ make the parts equal in size?

☐ check your answers?

☐ explain your answers?

- Grade 1 has two classes. Draw a line to divide the rectangular field into 2 equal parts. What shape is each part? What is the name of each equal part? Choose a word from the box at the right.

one half

one third

one fourth

- Explain how you could divide the same field into 2 equal parts that are a different shape. What shape is each part?

- There are four Grade 2 classes and four Grade 3 classes. Draw lines to divide each square field into 4 equal parts. Divide the two fields in different ways. What is the name of each equal part? Choose a word from the box above.

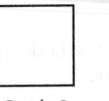

Grade 2   Grade 3

Reflect

Use a Tool How could you fold a piece of square paper to show that your squares have 4 equal parts?

©Curriculum Associates, LLC Copying is not permitted.

Glossary

AM morning, or the time from midnight until noon.

add to combine, or find the total.

addend a number being added.

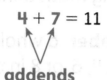

$$4 + 7 = 11$$

addends

analog clock a clock with an hour hand and a minute hand.

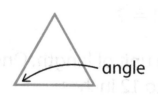

hour hand / minute hand

angle one of the corners of a shape where two sides meet.

angle

array a set of objects grouped in equal rows and equal columns.

bar graph a way to show data using bars.

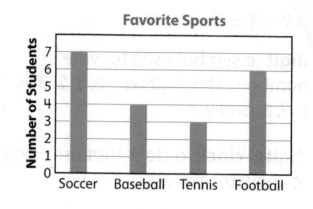

Favorite Sports

cent the smallest unit of money in the United States. One penny is one cent.

centimeter a unit of length. Your little finger is about 1 centimeter across.

column a top-to-bottom line of objects in an array.

compare to decide if one number is greater than (>), less than (<), or equal to (=) another number.

Glossary

D

data a set of collected information.

difference the result of subtraction.

$$9 - 3 = 6 \leftarrow \textbf{difference}$$

digit a symbol used to write numbers. The digits are 0, 1, 2, 3, 4, 5, 6, 7, 8, and 9.

digital clock a clock that uses digits to show the time.

dime a coin with a value of 10 cents.

dollar a unit of money equal to 100 cents.

E

equal (=) the same value or same amount.

3 + 1 is equal to 4

equation

equation a number sentence that uses an equal sign (=).

$3 + 5 = 8$ is an addition **equation**.

estimate (noun) a close guess made using math thinking.

estimate (verb) to make a close guess using math thinking.

even number a whole number that has a 0, 2, 4, 6, or 8 in the ones place. Even numbers are the numbers you say when you skip count by 2.

F

fact family a group of math facts that all use the same three numbers.

$$7 - 3 = 4$$
$$7 - 4 = 3$$
$$3 + 4 = 7$$
$$4 + 3 = 7$$

foot a unit of length. One foot is equal to 12 inches.

©Curriculum Associates, LLC   Copying is not permitted.

fourths the parts you get when you cut a whole into 4 equal parts.

fourths

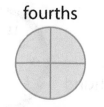

4 equal parts

G

greater than symbol (>) a symbol used to show that one number is more than another number.

6   4

6 is greater than 4.

H

halves the parts you get when you cut a whole into 2 equal parts.

halves

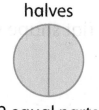

2 equal parts

hexagon a flat shape with exactly six sides and six angles.

hour a unit of time equal to 60 minutes.

hour hand the shorter hand on a clock. It shows hours.

hour hand

I

inch a unit of length. A quarter is about 1 inch across.

K

key an explanation of what each symbol in a pictograph represents.

L

length how long something is.

Glossary

less than symbol (<) a symbol used to show that one number is not as much as another number.

3   5

3 is less than 5.

line plot a graph that uses marks above a number line to show data.

Sea Lion Lengths

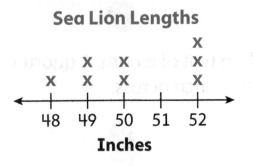

Inches

M

meter a unit of length. One meter is equal to 100 centimeters.

minute a unit of time equal to 60 seconds.

minute hand the longer hand on a clock. It shows minutes.

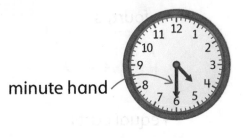

minute hand

N

nickel a coin with a value of 5 cents.

O

odd number a whole number that has a 1, 3, 5, 7, or 9 in the ones place.

P

PM the time from noon until midnight.

penny a coin with a value of 1 cent.

pentagon a flat shape with exactly five sides.

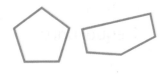

©Curriculum Associates, LLC   Copying is not permitted.

pictograph a way to show data using pictures.

Favorite Vegetables

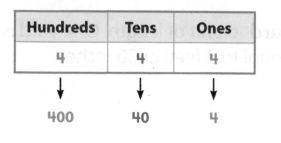

Carrots   Beans   Broccoli   Corn

Key: Each 😊 stands for 1 friend.

place value the value of a digit based on its place in a number.

Hundreds	Tens	Ones
4	4	4

↓ 400   ↓ 40   ↓ 4

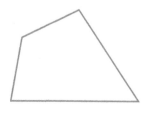

quadrilateral a flat shape with exactly four sides and four angles.

quarter a coin with a value of 25 cents.

rectangle a flat shape with 4 sides and four square corners.

regroup to put together or take apart tens and ones. For example, 12 ones is 1 ten and 2 ones.

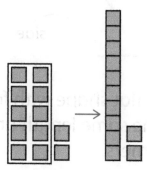

Regroup 12 ones as 1 ten and 2 ones

rhombus a flat shape with 4 sides and all sides the same length.

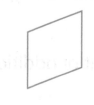

©Curriculum Associates, LLC   Copying is not permitted.

Glossary

row a side-to-side line of objects in an array.

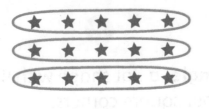

second a unit of time.

side one of the lines that make a two-dimensional shape.

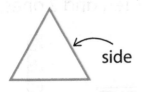

square a flat shape with four sides all the same length and four square corners.

subtract to take away, or to compare.

sum the result of addition.

$$9 + 3 = 12 \longleftarrow \textbf{sum}$$

thirds the parts you get when you cut a whole into three equal parts.

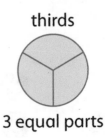

thirds

3 equal parts

triangle a flat shape with three straight sides and three angles.

yard a unit of length. One yard is equal to 3 feet, or 36 inches.

©Curriculum Associates, LLC Copying is not permitted.

Tennessee State Math Standards Coverage by *Ready* Instruction

The chart below correlates each Tennessee State Math Standard to the *Ready* Instruction lesson(s) that offer(s) comprehensive instruction on that standard. Use this chart to determine which lessons your students should complete based on their mastery of each standard.

Tennessee State Math Standards for Grade 2	*Ready* Instruction Lesson(s)
Operations and Algebraic Thinking (OA)	
A. Represent and solve problems involving addition and subtraction.	
2.OA.A.1 Add and subtract within 100 to solve one- and two-step contextual problems, with unknowns in all positions, involving situations of *add to, take from, put together/take apart,* and *compare.* Use objects, drawings, and equations with a symbol for the unknown number to represent the problem.	2, 6, 9, 21
B. Add and subtract within 30.	
2.OA.B.2 Fluently add and subtract within 30 using mental strategies. By the end of 2nd grade, know from memory all sums of two one-digit numbers and related subtraction facts.	1, 3
C. Work with equal groups of objects to gain foundations for multiplication.	
2.OA.C.3 Determine whether a group of objects (up to 20) has an odd or even number of members by pairing objects or counting them by 2s. Write an equation to express an even number as a sum of two equal addends.	4
2.OA.C.4 Use repeated addition to find the total number of objects arranged in rectangular arrays with up to 5 rows and up to 5 columns; write an equation to express the total as a sum of equal addends.	5
Number and Operations in Base Ten (NBT)	
A. Understand place value.	
2.NBT.A.1 Know that the three digits of a three-digit number represent amounts of hundreds, tens, and ones (e.g., 706 can be represented in multiple ways as 7 hundreds, 0 tens, and 6 ones; 706 ones; or 70 tens and 6 ones).	10
2.NBT.A.2 Count within 1000. Skip-count within 1000 by 5s, 10s, and 100s, starting from any number in its skip counting sequence.	5, 10, 24, 25
2.NBT.A.3 Read and write numbers to 1000 using standard form, word form, and expanded form.	11
2.NBT.A.4 Compare two three-digit numbers based on the meanings of the digits in each place and use the symbols >, =, and < to show the relationship.	12

The Standards for Mathematical Practice are integrated throughout the instructional lessons.
Tennessee State Math Standards ©2016. Tennessee State Board of Education. All rights reserved.

©Curriculum Associates, LLC   Copying is not permitted.

Number and Operations in Base Ten (NBT) *continued*

B. Use place value understanding and properties of operations to add and subtract.

2.NBT.B.5	Fluently add and subtract within 100 using properties of operations, strategies based on place value, and/or the relationship between addition and subtraction.	7–9
2.NBT.B.6	Add up to four two-digit numbers using properties of operations and strategies based on place value.	15
2.NBT.B.7	Add and subtract within 1000 using concrete models, drawings, strategies based on place value, properties of operations, and/or the relationship between addition and subtraction to explain the reasoning used.	13, 14
2.NBT.B.8	Mentally add 10 or 100 to a given number 100–900, and mentally subtract 10 or 100 from a given number 100–900.	7, 8
2.NBT.B.9	Explain why addition and subtraction strategies work using properties of operations and place value. (Explanations may include words, drawing, or objects.)	13, 14

Measurement and Data (MD)

A. Measure and estimate lengths in standard units.

2.MD.A.1	Measure the length of an object by selecting and using appropriate tools such as rulers, yardsticks, meter sticks, and measuring tapes.	16, 17
2.MD.A.2	Measure the length of an object using two different units of measure and describe how the two measurements relate to the size of the unit chosen.	18
2.MD.A.3	Estimate lengths using units of inches, feet, yards, centimeters, and meters.	19
2.MD.A.4	Measure to determine how much longer one object is than another and express the difference in terms of a standard unit of length.	20

B. Relate addition and subtraction to length.

2.MD.B.5	Add and subtract within 100 to solve contextual problems involving lengths that are given in the same units by using drawings and equations with a symbol for the unknown to represent the problem.	21
2.MD.B.6	Represent whole numbers as lengths from 0 on a number line and know that the points corresponding to the numbers on the number line are equally spaced. Use a number line to represent whole number sums and differences of lengths within 100.	21, 22

The Standards for Mathematical Practice are integrated throughout the instructional lessons.

©Curriculum Associates, LLC   Copying is not permitted.

Measurement and Data (MD) *continued*

C. Work with time and money.

2.MD.C.7 Tell and write time in quarter hours and to the nearest five minutes (in A.M. and P.M.) using analog and digital clocks.	24
2.MD.C.8 Solve contextual problems involving dollar bills, quarters, dimes, nickels, and pennies using ¢ and $ symbols appropriately.	25

D. Represent and interpret data.

2.MD.D.9 Generate measurement data by measuring lengths of several objects to the nearest whole unit. Show the measurements by making a line plot, where the horizontal scale is marked off in whole-number units.	22
2.MD.D.10 Draw a pictograph and a bar graph (with intervals of one) to represent a data set with up to four categories. Solve addition and subtraction problems related to the data in a graph.	23

Geometry (G)

A. Reason about shapes and their attributes.

2.G.A.1 Identify triangles, quadrilaterals, pentagons, hexagons, and cubes. Draw two-dimensional shapes having specified attributes (as determined directly or visually, not by measuring), such as a given number of angles or a given number of sides of equal length.	26
2.G.A.2 Partition a rectangle into rows and columns of same-sized squares and find the total number of squares.	27
2.G.A.3 Partition circles and rectangles into two, three, and four equal shares, describe the shares using the words *halves, thirds, fourths, half of, a third of,* and *a fourth of,* and describe the whole as *two halves, three thirds, four fourths.* Recognize that equal shares of identical wholes need not have the same shape.	28

The Standards for Mathematical Practice are integrated throughout the instructional lessons.

©Curriculum Associates, LLC   Copying is not permitted.

Acknowledgments

Illustration Credits

page 30: Rob McClurkan

page 146: Sam Valentino

page 240: Sam Valentino

page 243: Sam Valentino

page 274: Rob McClurkan

page 276: Sam Valentino

page 277: Sam Valentino

All other illustrations by Fian Arroyo.

Photography Credits

page 8: Natalia Korshunova/Shutterstock

page 48: Chesky/Shutterstock (robot)

page 48: stockernumber2/Shutterstock (shelf)

page 52: cameilia/Shutterstock (rocks)

page 52: Maxal Tamor/Shutterstock (trays)

page 54: 3DMAVR/Shutterstock (boxes)

page 54: vovan/Shutterstock (bolts)

page 55: konzeptm/Shutterstock

page 70: Tiplyashina Evgeniya/Shutterstock

page 106: Christophe Testi/Shutterstock

page 114: subin pumsom/Shutterstock

page 142: Sergio33/Shutterstock (chocolate chip cookie)

page 142: Bryan Solomon/Shutterstock (peanut butter cookie)

page 142: Danny Smythe/Shutterstock (oatmeal raisin cookie)

page 148: NataliTerr/Shutterstock

page 149: littleny/Shutterstock

page 161: Bragin Alexey/Shutterstock

page 167: Polryaz/Shutterstock (watch)

page 167: Maksim Toome/Shutterstock (car)

page 173: StockPhotosArt/Shutterstock (eraser)

page 173: Everything/Shutterstock (crayon)

page 173: Lucie Lang/Shutterstock (hair clip)

page 173: Enrique Ramos/Shutterstock (button)

page 174: schankz/Shutterstock

page 175: RTimages/Shutterstock

page 236: Enrique Ramos/Shutterstock

page 242: Kucher Serhii/Shutterstock (wooden hearts)

page 242: Simon Bratt/Shutterstock (wooden letters)

Background images used throughout lessons by Ortis/Shutterstock,
irin-k/Shutterstock, and Kritsada Namborisut/Shutterstock.